Collaboration *and* Taking Sides

Ronald Harwood's plays include *The Dresser*, *Another Time*, *Taking Sides*, *Quartet*, *Mahler's Conversion*, *An English Tragedy* and *Collaboration*. He is also the author of *Sir Donald Wolfit, CBE: His Life and Work in the Unfashionable Theatre*, and a history of theatre, *All the World's a Stage*. He is the editor of *The Faber Book of Theatre*. He was Visitor in Theatre at Balliol College, Oxford, President of English PEN from 1990 to 1993, and President of International PEN from 1993 to 1997. In 2000 he was awarded the Stefan Mitrov Ljubisa Prize for his contribution to European literature and human rights. He was Chairman of the Royal Society of Literature from 2001 to 2004 and elected President of the Royal Literary Fund in 2005. In 2002 he won the Academy Award for Best Adapted Screenplay for *The Pianist*, and in 2008 the BAFTA for his screenplay of *The Diving Bell and the Butterfly*. In 1996 he was appointed Chevalier de l'Ordre des Arts et des Lettres, and in 1999 he was awarded a CBE.

RONALD HARWOOD

Collaboration

and

Taking Sides

faber and faber

First published in 2008
by Faber and Faber Limited
3 Queen Square, London WC1N 3AU

Taking Sides first published in
Ronald Harwood: Plays Two, 1995,
and in a separate edition,
in the revised version here reprinted, 1995

Typeset by Country Setting, Kingsdown, Kent CT14 8ES
Printed in England by CPI Bookmarque, Croydon, Surrey

A CIP record for this book
is available from the British Library

978-0-571-24260-3

2 4 6 8 10 9 7 5 3 1

Contents

Collaboration
is a companion piece to *Taking Sides*

COLLABORATION

For George and Annabelle Weidenfeld

Collaboration was first presented at the Minerva Theatre, Chichester, in repertory with *Taking Sides*, on 16 July 2008. The cast was as follows:

Richard Strauss Michael Pennington
Pauline Strauss Isla Blair
Hans Hinkel Martin Hutson
Paul Adolph Pip Donaghy
Lotte Altman Sophie Roberts
Stefan Zweig David Horovitch

Directed by Philip Franks
Designed by Simon Higlett
Lighting by Mark Jonathan
Music by Matthew Scott
Sound by John A. Leonard

Characters

Richard Strauss

Pauline Strauss

Stefan Zweig

Lotte Altman

Hans Hinkel

Paul Adolph

The events take place between 1931 and 1948
in various locations

Act One

Strauss villa, Garmisch, July 1931.

Pauline Strauss, sixty-eight, a formidable woman, an ex-opera singer, sits reading. She is moved by what she reads and dabs at her eyes from time to time.

Richard Strauss, sixty-seven, enters, embattled, angry, frustrated. He stands staring at her.

Strauss I am dying.

Pauline (*barely raising her eyes*) Not again.

She continues to read.

Strauss Yes, scoff, scoff, but I tell you I may as well be dead.

No response from Pauline, who continues to read.

I am wandering in a desert. Sand, sand, sand!

He holds out his arms, makes a curious gesture twisting his wrists; then, in despair:

Oh God, what am I to do?

She looks at his shoes.

Pauline Did you wipe your feet?

Strauss Did I wipe my feet? Did I wipe my feet? Yes, I wiped my feet. First, on the damp doormat outside the door, then on the dry doormat also outside the door, and then I wiped them on the rubber doormat inside the door. I have obeyed your orders. Are you satisfied?

Pauline (*continuing to read*) Yes. Thank you.

Strauss (*rumbling*) Did I wipe my feet? I am not what they say I am. I am not the greatest living German composer. I am not a Titan or a demigod. I am a married man. Did I wipe my feet? (*About to explode.*) Shit, shit, shit!

No response; he paces, stops, turns to her.

Pauline, talk to me; have some sympathy, for pity's sake. I am suffocating.

Pauline I don't wish to count the number of times we've had this conversation. And I don't wish to count the number of times I have made the same suggestion. You don't listen so what's the –?

Strauss I need a conduit. I need a lifeline.

Pauline (*holds up the book to him*) I have given you my advice.

Strauss Yes, but it's bad advice.

Pauline How do you know until you've tried it? Telephone Kippenberg.

Strauss And what do I say?

Pauline You always know what to say.

Strauss And what will Kippenberg tell me? He'll tell me Stefan Zweig is the most successful author he publishes. His books sell in their thousands. Besides which, Zweig is very rich in his own right. His father left him a fortune.

Pauline So you keep saying, but what has that to do with anything?

Strauss Why would he want to supply me with an opera libretto? What possible incentive could he have?

Pauline Exactly the same as Hofmannsthal.

Strauss Hofmannsthal was a poet. Poets don't make money. Poets always need money. Hofmannsthal needed money.

Pauline You can't believe that was his only motive.

Strauss (*suddenly emotional*) Why did he have to go and die?

Pauline I'm sure he didn't do it on purpose.

Strauss paces.

Strauss The problem is Zweig is too important in his own right –

Pauline No more than Hofmannsthal –

Strauss (*ignoring her, overlapping*) He'll never say yes. Librettists are servants, librettists come very low in the opera hierarchy –

Pauline Nevertheless composers cannot do without them.

Strauss Shit, shit, shit!

Pauline I do wish you'd find something else to say.

Strauss This is the end. I may as well drink poison.

He is motionless, staring into space. She gazes at him. She relents, rises, goes to him, takes his hand.

Pauline Come, sweetheart, I'll make one last effort. I'll sit with you while you telephone Kippenberg.

Leads him to the telephone.

You can smoke a cigar, and, oh yes, please use the ashtray for your ash. That's what it's there for. The pattern on the carpet is turning a uniform grey.

She tugs at him to make him sit; he does not move.

9

Do it for me. Talk to Kippenberg. The worst that can happen is that Zweig says no.

Strauss villa, Garmisch, November, 1931.
   Light on Stefan Zweig, fifty, elegant and fastidious, but somewhat reserved and, at the moment, apprehensive.
   Strauss, now full of charm and bonhomie, walks towards him. They shake hands warmly.

Strauss No words can adequately express the pleasure your visit gives me. You have done me a great honour.

Zweig (*awkward, embarrassed*) No, no, the honour is mine. Entirely mine.

Strauss (*continuing to shake hands*) Ever since you replied to my letter so positively, I have not slept with excitement.

   Zweig tries unsuccessfully to withdraw his hand.

Zweig I would like – I wanted to – I simply must express in a modest way my affection and great admiration for you. That's why I –

Strauss (*still holding on*) How kind, how kind, you are so very welcome. Yes, welcome to Garmisch. Welcome to my humble home.

   Awkward moment for Zweig.

Zweig You must forgive me, but when I admire somebody I become deeply ill at ease.

Strauss (*letting go, full of good cheer*) Then I must stop talking like a small-town mayor greeting royalty at a railway station.

Strauss laughs; Zweig squeezes a smile.

My wife is longing to meet you. (*Calling.*) Pauline!

Zweig I have a gift for her. And for you.

He goes to his briefcase and takes from it a box wrapped in fancy paper and an envelope.

Strauss (*calling*) Pauline!

Pauline enters.

Pauline, may I present Stefan Zweig?

Zweig kisses her hand and bows, Austrian fashion.

Zweig Dear lady.

He presents the wrapped box to her.

Pauline Thank you. I am truly delighted to meet you. I never thought I would be so pleased to meet the man who made me cry so much.

Zweig Cry? Really?

Pauline I read your *Letter from an Unknown Woman* twice and I cried from beginning to end. Both times. (*To Strauss.*) I did, didn't I?

Strauss You certainly did. Both times. (*To Zweig.*) That's what you've done to us. She cried twice, I couldn't sleep, you have completely shattered our lives.

Zweig is pleased.

Pauline May I open this now?

Zweig Of course –

Pauline unwraps the parcel to reveal a box of chocolates.

Pauline *Mozartküchel*, our favourites –

Zweig Yes, Professor Kippenberg told me that you were particularly fond –

Pauline We will have them after luncheon. We shouldn't but we will. Thank you.

Zweig (*to Strauss*) And this is for you.

> *He hands him the envelope. Strauss opens it. He takes out a letter and his face lights up.*

Strauss God in heaven! Pauline, look, a letter from the Divine One. An even tastier *Mozartküchel*.

> *He shows her the letter.*

Zweig I read somewhere that you already have a Mozart letter, also to his cousin, but this one –

Strauss (*studying the letter*) But this one is magnificent. My dear Zweig, you are absurdly generous. No, no, I can't allow you to break up your collection, I can't possibly accept –

Zweig Please, it gives me enormous pleasure to present it to you.

Strauss How very kind. Thank you. (*He reads the letter, chuckles.*) The letter I have is so tame and inoffensive it could be read to a mixed audience of the Mozart Society. But this – (*Chuckles again.*) I would never dream of using such language in a letter. How unbelievably vulgar. Even I don't know what some of these words mean, and I'm a musician. Pauline, I'm not going to let you read this, you're not old enough. What a coarse frame of mind he must have had. Very disappointing.

Pauline Don't be so smug. You can be very coarse yourself sometimes.

Strauss Well then, at least I have something in common with Mozart. But why is it we always expect great artists to be great men?

Zweig I suppose because we're fascinated by the contradiction.

Pauline In my opinion great artists are seldom great men. And I've known one or two.

Awkward silence.

Come, let me show you to your room and you can unpack.

Zweig, embarrassed, doesn't move.

Strauss Is your luggage in the hall?

Zweig becomes even more awkward than before.

Zweig You must forgive me. I should have warned you. I – I am not a good house guest. I have booked into a hotel in Garmisch.

Strauss But it's November, all the hotels in Garmisch are closed –

Zweig An inn, it's an inn –

Pauline The inns in Garmisch are disgusting.

Zweig No, no, it's perfectly adequate –

Strauss We have a guest room here, modest but very comfortable –

Zweig Yes, you told me in your letter, but, you see, as a house guest, I always feel I'm disturbing my hosts –

Strauss Nonsense –

Zweig No, no, I'm as shy as a gazelle when staying in the house of a creative person. The feeling that I might disturb would be too oppressive.

They look at him blankly.

And I'm very sensitive to noise –

Strauss (*playful*) Noise? Noise? The only noise you'll hear is me on the piano playing my music – you regard that as noise?

Zweig No, no, no, no – the fact is, I wake early, and that's always an embarrassment. In somebody else's house.

Pauline Why?

Zweig I have to – I have to have coffee the moment I wake. If I'm in a strange house I never know whether I should get up and tiptoe down to the kitchen to make the coffee myself, or wait for the maid, or listen for someone stirring. I become very uneasy and, ergo, my day starts badly. At the inn, I simply ring the bell and someone appears. With my coffee.

Pauline Our maid arrives at seven.

Zweig I wake at six.

Pauline She lives in the next village. We could ask her to be here by six.

Zweig I've been known to wake at five.

Awkward silence.

I really don't want to disturb your arrangements.

Another awkward silence.

I should warn you, a psychologist friend told me I'm a neurotic. I think he meant it as a joke but sometimes I'm not so sure.

He tries to smile.

Strauss If that was Freud, beware. He never jokes.

Zweig No, no, no, no, no. I know Freud but he certainly hasn't analysed me.

Pauline Be grateful for small mercies.

Strauss Well. All artists are neurotic.

Pauline (*with feeling*) How very true. (*Going.*) So. I will leave you artists to it. Thank you for the chocolates.

She goes. Immediately:

Strauss My dear Zweig, I can't wait any longer. You have an idea for an opera. Tell me.

Zweig (*taken aback*) Yes, yes. In fact, I – I – I have two ideas, but –

Strauss Better and better. Let me hear both of them.

Zweig I think – I believe – it would be easier for me if you could first give me some notion of the sort of thing you are looking for.

Strauss I am looking for an opera! My mouth is filled with sand for want of a subject. I haven't written an opera since *Arabella*. That's three years ago. I have music choking my lungs and no way to exhale it. I have notes swirling in my head, like a – like a sandstorm. I must find a subject for an opera or die.

Zweig I want to be sure I am not wasting your time.

Strauss You won't be wasting my time –

Zweig Nevertheless, can't you give me some idea –?

Strauss Let me make a confession. At the age I am, sixty-seven, a composer's musical inspiration no longer possesses, what shall I call it, its pristine power? I know I won't ever again compose anything like *Till Eulenspiegel* or *Rosenkavalier* because music, especially pure music, requires an extreme measure of creative freshness. But the word can still inspire me, something tangible, like scaffolding on which I can build. That's why I've been devoting myself to opera these last years. Yes, yes, I know, opera as an art form is dead. That devil Wagner was such a gigantic peak, that nobody can rise higher. (*He grins.*) But I solved the problem by making a detour round him.

He makes a gesture as if now handing over to Zweig.

Zweig I'm not sure that helps –

Strauss All right, all right. I'll try to explain something else to you. Let me see if I can put you at your ease. (*Suddenly.*) Do you know what a dowser is?

Zweig A dowser, of course, a – a water-diviner.

Strauss Exactly. A dowser walks around a field with a forked stick, looking for water. And when the stick is above the hidden water the dowser's arms stiffen and the stick turns downwards. (*He mimes, making the odd gesture with his wrists.*) I saw it done once, not long ago, in a travelogue, a film – you know the sort of thing, American, where it always ends with the sun sinking slowly in the west. And I thought it the most perfect metaphor for my creative process, which is precisely like dowsing. You will tell me an idea and I will know at once if it is something for an opera I can compose, because that forked stick inside me turns downwards. I know when I have divined the subject that will inspire my music. If I don't respond to your ideas, I remain limp. But just remember it has nothing to do with you but only with me, with the forked stick inside me. You understand?

Zweig Yes. I hope so. Thank you.

Strauss So, lead me across the barren field and let me dowse.

A brief silence.

Zweig But – but are you not able to give me just a little guidance?

Strauss (*exasperated*) Yes, yes, yes, all right! A woman!

Zweig A woman?

Strauss That's what I want from you.

Zweig I'm not sure I understand –

Strauss No one in the world writes about women better than you. So. From the author of *Twenty-Four Hours in a Woman's Life*, and your magnificent *Fouché*, I want a woman!

Zweig Could you – could you be a little more explicit?

Strauss Of all the women in all my operas I lack a type that I would love to set to music for the stage.

Zweig And what type is that?

Strauss The woman adventurer. The *grande dame* as spy. A female racketeer – yes, that's what I'm after, a female racketeer. I believe that to be a very modern concept. And I never did agree with poor old Hofmannsthal, who thought that an intelligent play about intrigue is no longer acceptable today. I said it depends on what it is and how it is done.

Zweig That's true of all art. But – (*Goes to his briefcase, takes out a notebook.*) I'm not sure I can supply a female racketeer, I –

Strauss For God's sake, put me out of my misery, Zweig, talk to me. Tell me your thoughts, tell me your ideas. What sweet aromas arise from your creative spring?

Zweig takes a deep breath.

Zweig I'm going to dive straight in.

Strauss Good.

Silence.

Zweig You must understand that I have been in awe of you all my life and so I am naturally –

Strauss Please, Zweig, plunge!

Zweig summons his courage.

Zweig The first of my ideas is to me the more significant and important. (*An announcement.*) A dancing pantomime in the grand style.

Strauss shuts his eyes.

Please don't reject the idea out of hand. I envisage a work, universally understandable, playable on every stage in the world, in all languages, before any audience, highbrow or lowbrow, a work that comprises all the contrasts of the arts – tragic, light-hearted, Apollonian, Dionysian – a work in which the world's greatest living composer, you, Richard Strauss, can reach the highest peak of his art.

Strauss remains motionless.

Now. Don't be misled by the term dancing pantomime. I am not suggesting a minor work. (*Growing more passionate.*) I conceive it as a pantomime only broken once by the human voice when it reaches its internal peak. And I visualise a fearsome beauty when the audience, until then wholly immersed in the language of musical instruments, is suddenly shaken by hearing that most holy and sublime of all instruments, the human voice.

Strauss looks as if he may be asleep; silence.

My other idea – (*He breaks off, collects his thoughts.*) Of course you know the works of Ben Jonson.

No response.

Volpone is his best known play, I did a version of my own, I think in your letter you said you saw it, or read it; well, it was not unsuccessful. There's another of his plays that might provide the basis for an opera. It's called *Epicoene, or The Silent Woman.*

No response.

It's a comedy in which Jonson combined two themes brilliantly. The central plot is of a foolish old man who marries only to discover, to his intense relief, that the marriage is null and void because the bride turns out to be a young man.

Strauss's eyes snap open.

At the same time, there's a concept of a misanthrope who hates noise, united to a mouse-like girl who immediately after the ceremony turns into a virago –

Strauss's eyes bulge; he pretends to hyperventilate.

Dr Strauss, what's the matter, are you ill? Shall I call your wife?

Strauss (*still acting, staggers*) Water. Water.

Zweig (*looking around*) Is there a jug here? Where do I find –?

Strauss (*stopping his performance*) No, no, you idiot! My God, you're more stupid than a viola player!

(*Miming the dowser.*) Water! Water! (*Joyous.*) Water! (*Laughs delightedly, repeats the dowsing action several times.*) Water!

Zweig suddenly understands and smiles.

Zweig's villa, Salzburg, June 1932.
Strauss sits beside Pauline and both listen to Zweig reading from a typescript.
In the background, also seated, Lotte Altmann, twenty-four, a withdrawn, slender, self-effacing woman.

Zweig (*reading*) And then I thought he might sing something along these lines, 'How beautiful music is, how really beautiful but only when it is over.'

Strauss chuckles.

'How wonderful is a young silent woman, how really wonderful, but only when she is the wife of somebody else! How beautiful is life, how beautiful, but only when one knows how to live it. I never felt so happy.' Now, perhaps I thought he might light his pipe. He goes on – I imagine all this to be part of the final aria – 'Oh, I feel indescribably well, and quiet, simply quiet.' Then I thought he should emit a long, long sigh, a musical sigh. The last notes sound. And the curtain falls. Finis.

A brief silence. Strauss and Pauline rise and applaud. Lotte slips away.

Strauss (*standing*) Bravi! Bravi! Absolutely excellent, as they say in *Cosi fan tutte*!

Pauline Yes, yes, dear Herr Zweig, it's quite wonderful. I wish I was still young enough to sing Aminta.

Strauss Oh, my warmest, warmest congratulations –

Zweig I incorporated most of your suggestions, our meetings were so useful to me, but remember it's only a synopsis –

Strauss A synopsis? It's the finished article! There's nothing to criticise, I don't want to change a single thing –

Zweig (*pleased*) Really?

Strauss My instinct tells me that perhaps a few cuts may be needed –

Zweig (*alarmed*) What cuts?

Strauss There's no hurry, and we don't have to decide now about the ending –

Zweig What's wrong with the ending?

Strauss Nothing, nothing, it's all absolutely excellent. Some advice, my dear Zweig –

Zweig Yes?

Strauss After the opera is shown to the public, take a three year round-the-world trip.

Zweig Why?

Strauss To escape my libretto-hungry colleagues. For my own part, I've never encountered anything so perfect. I just know it will be easy for me to set to music. But may we walk? Get some air? My head is coming off with excitement.

He takes Zweig's arm.

I cannot tell you how grateful I am.

They go.

Pauline Richard! Richard! Am I to be left alone?

Lotte appears with a tea tray and, seeing only Pauline, stops dead.

Lotte Oh.

Pauline Yes. When artists talk art, they lose their manners. They've gone out for a walk. It's really too bad.

Lotte Should we wait for them?

Pauline No.

Lotte lays down the tray.

And you say Frau Zweig knew we were coming?

Lotte Yes.

Pauline But she's in Vienna.

Lotte Yes.

Pauline When will she be back?

Lotte I'm – I'm not sure.

Pauline watches her. Lotte pours the tea and is about to add a slice of lemon.

Pauline No. No lemon. I take milk in my tea, like the English.

Lotte (*a little distressed*) Yes, yes, I'm sorry, I have milk.

Lotte pours the milk and then the tea, brings it to her.

Pauline You've already put the milk in.

Lotte Yes. You said. Like the English.

Pauline In England only the lower classes put the milk in first.

Lotte Oh.

Pauline The gentry add their own milk after the tea is poured. In that way, one can be certain one has exactly the right amount of milk to one's taste.

Lotte I'll get another cup –

Pauline No, it's still drinkable.

Lotte I can easily –

Pauline (*sharp*) No. (*She sips her tea.*) Vienna.

Lotte Yes.

Pauline And you are the secretary.

Lotte Yes.

Pauline And she has left you alone with Herr Zweig?

Lotte (*surprised by the question*) Yes.

Pauline Do you live here in the villa?

Lotte Oh, no.

Pauline But you work here.

Lotte Yes.

Pauline You live in the town.

Lotte Yes. In Salzburg.

Pauline Tell me your name again.

Lotte Charlotte Altmann. But people call me Lotte.

Pauline 'But people call me Lotte.' Sounds like an aria.

  Awkward silence.

Did you enjoy hearing the synopsis read?

Lotte Oh, yes. Herr Zweig has such a beauti— (*Brief hesitation.*) He reads very well.

Awkward pause.

Pauline I expect you typed it.

Lotte Yes.

Pauline On a typewriter.

Lotte Yes.

Pauline And do you like it, the synopsis?

Lotte Oh yes, very much.

Awkward silence. The sound of Strauss's laugh.

Pauline Ah, the artists are returning. You don't have to stay. You may go and do your work.

Lotte leaves quickly as Strauss and Zweig return, arm in arm.

Strauss Pauline, come outside and rejoice in the views, you can see Berchtesgaden –

Pauline You left me alone –

Zweig Dear lady, I apologise, how very thoughtless, I'm so sorry –

Pauline No matter. The secretary girl brought me tea.

Zweig Oh, good –

Strauss There is nothing so glorious in all Europe as the sight of the Obersalzburg thrusting into the clear, blue Austrian sky, and the perpetual snow-capped –

Pauline (*interrupting, to Strauss*) I haven't time to listen to poetry or to look at the mountains. I'm going into the town. I have some shopping to do. Then I will come back

24

to fetch you. (*To Zweig.*) Please see that he is ready by no later than five o'clock. We have to be in Vienna in time for the sleeper to Milan. We are going on to Como.

Zweig Yes, your husband said –

She starts to go but stops.

Pauline (*pointedly*) Oh. And please give my warmest regards to Frau Zweig.

She goes.
Strauss takes up the typescript of the synopsis, reads and chuckles.

Zweig And you – you really like it?

Strauss Like it? I am completely overwhelmed by it. When can you start on Act One?

Zweig (*avoiding an answer*) Yes, well, I – I will need advice.

Strauss About what?

Zweig I have a sort of block.

Strauss A writer's block? Heaven forbid –

Zweig No, no, I've never had that.

Strauss What then?

Zweig It has to do with operatic form.

Strauss Explain.

Zweig This will sound ridiculously naive to you, but when I come to face the reality of setting down the libretto, I know I will have to confront what is to me now an insoluble problem.

Strauss No problem in music is insoluble.

Zweig I hope you are right. Of course, in order to tell the story I can supply lyrics for the arias, duets, trios and so on, but what worries me are the connecting passages.

Strauss Why?

Zweig To put it bluntly: should I employ the concept of recitative or – or spoken dialogue in prose, as if in a play?

Strauss I see! Good, good. This is not a problem. And if it is, it's easily solved. *Recitativo secco* is not my cup of tea.

Zweig Never?

Strauss Never. I'll tell you why. Its diatonic and harmonic Mozartian simplicity simply does not fit my musical style. So, you write the dialogue in prose and then let me decide. I'll give you an example. (*Tries to remember.*) What's that play of yours I like so much?

Zweig Difficult for me to say –

Strauss About the prophet –

Zweig *Jeremiah*.

Strauss Exactly. The last lines, perfect. I committed them to memory. 'One can kill men but not the God that resides within them. One can enslave a people, but never its spirit.' Lines like that should be spoken not sung. And just remember, I don't compose long melodies like Mozart. I never get beyond short themes. But what I can do is use such a theme, paraphrase it, extract every ounce that's in it, and I don't think there's anybody alive who can match me at that. (*He beams.*) So. When can you deliver –?

Zweig You have just touched on the heart of my problem. I understand that a heroic or lyrical opera demands music throughout, but, even in our sort of light opera, with such a mixture of moods, I still think it may need a musical accompaniment. No, I don't mean Mozart on the clavichord, that would smack a little too much of lavender, but what about a very light accompaniment on instruments accented more sharply than the clavichord? Flute, saxophone, drum, a modern scansion. It would be something entirely new, something contemporary, so that you, better than anyone else, could show the young how to renew and update the recitative. The critics will love it. They love anything new.

Strauss New is not necessarily good.

Zweig The critics don't always know that.

Strauss I'll think about it. But my advice is write the dialogue in prose and –

Zweig And there are, as you said, other things we need to discuss –

Strauss There is nothing to discuss. This synopsis of yours tells me that *The Silent Woman* is a born comic opera, a comedy equal to the best of its kind. This demands music more than even *Figaro* or *The Barber of Seville*. You know what I love most about you? You are a born storyteller. In all art, novels, plays, painting, opera, there is nothing more important than the story. In music, each note must lead the listener forward, telling the story. And then, and then, and then? You, Zweig, always make one impatient to know what's going to happen next. When can I expect the first act?

Zweig, embarrassed, affects an ineffectual laugh, prevaricating.

What's so funny?

Zweig It's odd.

Strauss What is?

Zweig Whenever anyone says 'and then', a cheap line from a bad play comes into my mind. I once contemplated writing a biography of Anne Boleyn and, during my researches, stumbled across an indifferent play about her. In the last scene, just before she's to be executed, the Archbishop visits her. She asks him what will happen, she wants him to describe in precise detail her journey from her cell to the scaffold so she can be prepared. The Archbishop says, 'They will come here and fetch you.' 'And then?' she asks. And then, and then? Each time she asks the question 'And then?' he takes her on to the next step, step by step, until that moment when her head is laid on the block. The Archbishop says, 'And then the executioner will raise his axe.' She asks, 'And then?' The Archbishop does not reply. And so very slowly she supplies the answer herself. 'And then,' she says, 'after the axe falls, I shall be wiser than you, My Lord Archbishop.' It's a terrible line but it haunts me. 'I shall be wiser than you, My Lord Archbishop.'

Strauss (*a little bemused*) But what has this to do with our project?

Zweig I was wondering if composers – if you – are ever haunted by other composers' bad tunes?

Strauss No. When can you send me the first act?

Silence.

Zweig (*cornered*) I'd better confess.

Strauss What?

Zweig I – I have a bad conscience. I – I – I'm not sure I can begin work at once –

Strauss (*appalled*) But you must –

Zweig The fact is I'm trying to finish my biography of Marie Antoinette –

Strauss We all know how she ended, so let's start on this.

Zweig And another thing. I have to work on a lecture I'm to give in Italy. And in Italian, may Dante forgive me. The time is not right. I need a period of – I need the – the right – élan –

Strauss But can't you see the state I'm in? I can't wait to work on it. Intensively.

Zweig It's difficult for me to find the enthusiasm when I am so weighed down by –

Strauss I must start work now, at once, immediately. In the beginning it takes a while for me to get going and to find the right style. But as soon as I've drafted half an act, the imagination runs by itself.

Zweig (*steely; firm*) I have to finish my book.

Silence.

Strauss Give me some idea of when that will be.

Zweig A month. No more.

Strauss A whole month?

Zweig Yes.

Silence.

Strauss I read recently *Cagliostro* by Alexandre Dumas. Did you know that several times he mentions Marie Antoinette's virginity?

Zweig Yes.

Silence.

Strauss Are you often drawn to women who have their heads chopped off?

Zweig No, not often.

Silence.

Strauss I want to tell you something important. I am not a sentimental man. I have tried to keep sentiment out of my music and out of my life. Treacle is not to my liking. Nevertheless, I feel obliged to say that I have never felt more at ease, more able to say what I feel, more at one with a colleague than I do with you.

Zweig (*surprised and flattered*) Oh. Thank you.

Strauss Don't thank me. I'm not given easily to intimate friendships. I seem to have no need of them. Perhaps it's because for most of my life I have lived such a disciplined, solitary life. Nothing demonic. No exaltation. No depression, no desperation. I sit down at nine, pick up where I left off the day before, write the first sketch in pencil, the piano score in ink, and I go on without pause until noon. In the afternoon I play skat, and then I might transfer two or three pages to the final score. And that's how it's been for most of my life. And even when I conduct an orchestra, it's not as if I'm in contact with individuals. But it has been different working with you. These past months, after all the letters we've exchanged and our many meetings, it feels odd to me at my age to have made a new friend, a real friend.

Zweig You touch me deeply –

Strauss Though when I met you, you were not what I expected.

Zweig What did you expect?

Strauss Someone very haughty and imperious.

Zweig How odd, I thought you'd be like that, too.

Strauss Me? Don't be ridiculous, I come from peasant stock, how could I be haughty and imperious?

Zweig I have no doubt my ancestors were peasants, too –

Strauss Perhaps that's what we have in common. And an awareness of the distance we have travelled. We appreciate how privileged we are. We are not citizens of any particular country, but of – all right, I'll be haughty and imperious – citizens of the world. That is the passport our gifts have conferred on us.

Zweig I'm sure in your case that's certainly true. Your music is played everywhere. But as far as I'm concerned – I'm not being falsely modest, believe me – I think probably I belong only to Europe.

Strauss (*amused*) Only!

Zweig I travel a great deal but I know I can't live long separated from my cultural roots. It's curious, but I feel instantly at home anywhere on this continent, I simply love its old earth. Everything I hold dear – music, literature, the theatre, scholarship, science – finds light in Europe, for the most part free of confinement and prejudice. Yes, free. I hold human freedom and, of course, the freedom of expression to be the paramount ideal. I've often felt that being a European was a sort of mission.

Strauss Yes, yes, I have no doubt you have been sent to me from Heaven.

Zweig Now you embarrass me –

Strauss And it occurred to me that I have never asked about your family or confided in you about mine. How long have you been married?

Zweig (*a smile*) Officially, fifteen years.

Strauss Children?

Zweig No.

Strauss I should like to meet your wife.

No response.

Pauline and I will have been married thirty-three years in September. (*Haltingly.*) We have one son. Franz. He married a Jewess but we are very fond of her. Alice Grab. Her father's a well-to-do merchant. In fact, Alice is one of the few people I am really devoted to. Very pretty. Blonde. Highly intelligent. She has given us two delightful grandchildren.

Brief silence.

As you see, it's a struggle for me to talk intimately. Writers need conversation. Composers need silence. Although it's true Offenbach used to compose in bed with his friends sitting around, chatting and gossiping, eating croissants and drinking coffee. Inconceivable to me. But then he was French.

Zweig I, too, like solitude and silence.

Strauss But your soirées and parties are always in the papers. You seem to know everybody who is anybody.

Zweig That's more to my wife's liking than mine. She loves the social whirl.

Strauss And you don't?

Zweig I find it a distraction.

Strauss Do you make friends easily?

Zweig I make acquaintances easily.

Silence.

Strauss Before I met you, I was closer to Hofmannsthal than any other man I have known. Please don't think this insensitive of me, but I dreamed of him the other night. I dreamed I was having breakfast in the house of a great lord who was however not there. Hofmannsthal entered and said to me, 'I have a one-act opera text for you: very tender – with nymphs.'

He smiles sadly at the memory.

Zweig He was a great poet.

Strauss (*with difficulty*) Zweig, I want us to go on collaborating until we are so old we cannot remember each other's names. Or our own. (*Zweig smiles.*) I mean it. You have given me the confidence to believe that together we may create masterpieces.

Zweig I don't know about masterpieces but – I – I sometimes have to pinch myself to realise that I am actually collaborating with the composer of *Rosenkavalier* – (*Breaks off.*) I, too, have confidence in our future. Together.

Strauss is pleased. Silence.

Strauss Oh yes, about terms. Will it suit you if we now draw up a formal agreement?

Zweig Of course.

Strauss For you, twenty-five per cent royalties from stage productions, twenty per cent from the book and also of the piano score. Is that agreeable?

Zweig More than generous.

Strauss No, not generous, standard. I will ask my lawyer to draw up the contract. And I believe it will be necessary for you to join the Association of German Composers in Berlin to insure that you'll receive your share from concert performances of fragments with lyrics from our opera. Also from records and films.

Zweig Thank you, I'll ask Fräulein Altmann to obtain the forms.

Silence.

Strauss A month.

Zweig What?

Strauss To finish Anne Boleyn.

Zweig Marie Antoinette.

Strauss Yes. Would it make things easier if I came to visit you again, here in Salzburg?

Zweig When?

Strauss After you've finished the draft of Act One, which you will start in a month, you say. Once you've sent me the draft we'll need more face-to-face meetings. I'll arrange my affairs so that I can come here for a week or two.

Zweig I don't want to put you to trouble.

Strauss (*a twinkle*) I'll stay at an inn.

They smile.

I have a feeling this will be the most productive period of our lives.

ACT ONE

Zweig's villa, Salzburg, April 1933.
The sound of terrified crying.
Lotte enters, sobbing, near to hysteria. Her nose is
bleeding, her hair dishevelled, mud on her skirt.
Zweig hurries to her.

Zweig Fräulein Altmann, what's happened to you? Calm
down, tell me. Sit –

He finds brandy and pours some for her.

Drink this –

She shakes her head.

Drink it.

She manages a small swallow.

Breathe deeply and calm down.

She struggles for control.

Good.

She becomes calmer.

Now, tell me what has happened.

Slowly, she more or less gains a fragile control of
herself.

Lotte (*tears returning*) Two men – I was talking to Leah
Neumann – I was so frightened – Leah ran off, she fell –
they –

She cries again.

Zweig Start at the beginning. Where were you, what
were you doing?

Lotte I – I went into town, to the post office, to mail Act
Two to Dr Strauss. When I came out, I saw Leah, she'd

been buying a hat. We stopped to talk. Then, two men – boys –

She falls silent, fighting tears.

Zweig Who were they?

Lotte They weren't local, they may have been German –

Zweig No, they can't have been German, the Nazis have closed the border –

Lotte I don't know, the older one said, 'Look! Two of them!' And then they stood either side of us and started chanting –

Zweig Were they drunk?

Lotte No, no – (*In a rush.*) And no one stopped to help us, no one, there was even a policeman, but he just walked on –

Zweig You said they were chanting, what did they chant?

She shakes her head.

Tell me.

Continues to shake her head.

Tell me.

She summons courage.

Lotte (*barely audible*) 'Whores, whores, Jewish whores.'

Silence.

Zweig What did you do?

Lotte Just stood, frozen, terrified. The older boy had something in his hand, a stone maybe, something, I don't know, whatever it was he threw it, hit Leah on her arm. She screamed and so did I. We both started to run, she one way, I the other, but the younger boy, he must have been fourteen, fifteen, he stood in my path and I ran into him, I couldn't stop myself. I fell over and hit my nose. I thought my head was going to explode. I started to bleed, I could taste the blood. They laughed. And then I saw Leah fall, but they were only interested in me, they stood over me, shouting the same thing again and again – (*Barely audible.*) 'Whore – whore – Jewish whore.' (*She sobs.*) People just watched – and the policeman walked by –

Zweig It's over now. They were just louts. It won't happen again.

She suddenly puts her arms round Zweig's waist and clings to him. At first he is tense, then gradually relaxes, strokes her hair.

Gently he loosens her embrace, kneels, takes out a handkerchief and wipes her nose clean. They stare at each other, long and hard. He kisses her gently on the forehead. She runs from the room.

Strauss villa, Garmisch, and Zweig villa, Salzburg, April 1933.

In Garmisch, Pauline holds the telephone receiver over the piano where Strauss plays and sings from the end of Act One of The Silent Woman.

In Salzburg, Zweig holds his telephone receiver and listens. Lotte stands beside him, craning to hear. After a moment, he puts his arm around her shoulders, ostensibly to draw her closer to the receiver but it is tantamount to an embrace.

Strauss plays and sings in that particularly unmusical tone of conductors and composers, a snatch from the

*love duet between Henry and Aminta ending with
Henry's 'Oh, Kind, wie glücklich machst du mich!'*

Strauss (*calling out to the telephone*) Now, Henry and
Aminta hold each other in a tight embrace. And –

*He plays on, calling out the orchestration, and then
suddenly breaks off.*

(*Shouting into the telephone.*) That's as far as I've got.

End of Act One.

Act Two

Zweig's villa, Salzburg, April 1933.
  *Zweig, in a highly charged state, close to incoherence,
pacing. Strauss and Pauline watch him, alarmed.*

Zweig Just imagine getting such a thing wrong in a
broadcast, not by some nonentity but by Goebbels
himself – Goebbels, Josef Goebbels, Minister of
Propaganda, getting it wrong, he did not say Arnold
Zweig, he simply said Zweig and quoted that passage, it's
an infamous, vicious passage for God's sake, ill-written,
and profoundly anti-Nazi, and he just said by Zweig, not
Arnold Zweig, simply Zweig, so, of course, people will
think it's me, I have to have a correction printed, they
have to print a correction –

Pauline I can understand you objecting because it's ill-
written, but anti-Nazi –

Zweig Forgive me but that's not the point. The passage
incites violence. I disassociate myself from violence at all
times, no matter how foul the enemy. The ends do not
justify the means, that way lies death and destruction –

  *He runs out of steam, stops pacing, stands, trying to
  catch his breath, a hand to his forehead. After a
  moment:*

Strauss Please, dear friend, listen to me calmly. I will be
in touch with important friends, and I will make sure a
retraction is printed. In all modesty, I believe I have some
influence – after all, the border is closed with Austria but

39

we are here in your home in Salzburg. Believe me, I have influence –

Zweig Thank you, thank you, but I don't think you fully understand. They are burning books –

Pauline Yes, we know –

Zweig Everything we hold dear is now valueless. You have a government of gangsters – and who cares, who protests? The outside world says it's happening beyond their borders, it's not their concern. But it is, it's everyone's concern. These criminals move slowly, slowly, bit by bit, one drop of poison at a time, until all the world will perish. Look – (*Opens his briefcase, takes from it charred remains of a book.*) A student rescued this from the execution. It's a book I wrote years ago, *The Tide of Fortune*. What title could be more apt? (*Holds the book high.*) I regard it as an honour to be allowed to share the fate of the total destruction of our literary heritage. A badge of honour. (*He becomes still, stares into space, slowly lowers the book.*) Yes, poison. Everything is poisoned. I can't even look at the mountains any more.

Pauline But why not?

Zweig Because his house is there. In Berchtesgaden. I feel his eyes on me. I feel the violence threatening. And I am overcome by unbearable heat.

Strauss and Pauline exchange a look of concern.

(*A little more calmly.*) I haven't written a word since all this happened.

Strauss (*trying to lighten the mood*) Not me. I am busily at work, just as I was a week after the outbreak of the Great War. By the way, the draft of Act One is now copied in final form.

Zweig Yes, history shows that in times of greatest unrest artists work with greatest concentration.

Strauss I work with greatest concentration no matter what the circumstances. (*He laughs, once more trying to lighten the mood.*)

Zweig (*erupting*) God, politics disgust me! And why are politicians always so shabby and dishonest? Deception is their watchword. Truth is their greatest enemy. I don't want to be drawn into their nightmares. I have enough of my own. I have to resist with all my strength. But one has to keep on and on defending oneself.

Pauline I'd like to come face to face with Dr Goebbels. I'd tell him a thing or two. I'd fix him.

Strauss Of that I have no doubt. But, Zweig, it will all blow over, take my word for it. It can't last. The Nazis will never be able to practise what they preach.

Brief silence.

Zweig I have always believed that politics pass but the arts live on. Now I must confess that my faith has been shaken.

Strauss Look on the bright side. They understand the importance of the arts. They intend to support culture. German culture.

Zweig No. They intend to control culture. And when governments control the arts, artists become robots unless they have the courage to –

He breaks off.

Pauline To do what?

Zweig To act out of a moral imperative. (*Lost for a moment.*) Strange how the chaos that engulfs us seems

41

to be mirrored in my private life. I have something to tell you which I hope won't be distressing. (*After a brief moment.*) My wife and I have parted.

Strauss My dear Zweig.

Zweig You and I talked once of the need for silence and solitude. For some time now, I have felt – imprisoned, I don't know how else to describe it. A feeling of being suffocated. Yes, yes, I know, it sounds like a line from a cheap romantic novel, but I have craved to live more and more in my own world, at moments of my own choosing. I had to take drastic action. I much regret causing pain, but – (*Breaks off.*) I just needed to unburden. You are the first people I've told. Forgive me. But I believe we are friends and I wanted you to know. Also to avoid embarrassment.

Strauss Thank you.

Pauline Is there someone else in your life?

Strauss looks daggers at her. After a moment:

Zweig There may be.

Strauss (*as ever trying to lighten the mood*) I can do nothing for your private affairs, my dear Zweig. But as regards this matter with Goebbels, please leave that to me and put it from your mind.

Pauline It will end happily, I feel it. The difference in your ages is irrelevant. Fräulein Altmann is devoted to you.

Zweig gives her a startled look. Strauss indicates secretly to Pauline that she should leave them.

If you want me to go, say so. Don't dismiss me like a servant. (*She is about to go, stops. To Zweig.*) I will walk in your garden. I won't look at the mountains. But my husband is right. It will all blow over. And I'm sure you'll be very happy. Fräulein Altmann, I suspect, has a very quiet soul.

She goes. Silence.

Strauss My wife – my wife is very perceptive, but she can be sometimes too direct. However, I would be nothing without her. She has made my life possible. If it wasn't for her we would not be working together. She admires you more than I can say.

Zweig And I have great affection for her –

Strauss She was a soprano. Very good. But singers seldom understand art. Especially sopranos. And tenors. And baritones. By the way, I've given the soprano who'll sing Aminta some hard nuts to crack. Let her struggle like hell to get what's in them. (*He chuckles with relish.*) Zweig, I want to help you find your way back to work. Allow me to speak frankly. You feel oppressed privately and publicly. But believe me, work is the only antidote. We must go on. We must find a new subject for a grand opera, something spectacular. That will be our answer to all this madness. For my own part, I become desperate when idle.

Zweig But your creativity is inexhaustible. I'm not so sure about mine.

Strauss Find another subject for an opera, I implore you, I beg you. I'd go down on my knees if it weren't for my rheumatism.

Zweig smiles.

And I make you this solemn promise. I will never co-operate with the Nazis. And I will never desert you. Never.

Strauss villa, Garmisch, November 1933.

The Hitler salute from Hans Hinkel, aged thirty-three, in a Propaganda Ministry uniform. He is a man of immense charm who smiles a great deal.

Strauss responds with a half-hearted salute. Pauline remains still.

Hinkel Hinkel. State Commissioner, Reich Chamber of Culture. I was so pleased to receive your invitation. Thank you. It is such a great honour to meet you at last.

Pauline Did you wipe your feet?

Hinkel is a little taken aback.

Hinkel Yes.

Strauss (*amused*) On all three mats?

Hinkel thinks about it.

Hinkel Yes.

Strauss Then all is well. Thank you for coming so promptly.

Hinkel How could I refuse an invitation from the greatest living German composer? I was pleased to take this opportunity to meet you because –

Pauline (*interrupting*) My husband explained the problem in his letter.

Hinkel Yes, the Zweig business.

Pauline The Arnold Zweig business.

Hinkel I'm not sure I understand the fuss. Two Jew writers called Zweig, it's easy to make a mistake.

Strauss Stefan Zweig is one of the foremost writers in the German language. I know nothing of the other man.

44

Hinkel He is a Jew Communist.

Strauss (*waving the information aside*) The mistake caused my collaborator Stefan Zweig immense trouble.

Hinkel I'm not sure what it is you want me to do –

Strauss I will tell you what I've already done. I contacted my friend Hugo Rasch, music editor of the *Völkischer Beobachter*. He has promised to do everything he can with his chief, Rosenberg, to get an apology and a retraction published.

Hinkel (*a broad smile*) Then I am superfluous.

Strauss hesitates, but Pauline steps in.

Pauline No. My husband thinks Dr Goebbels should apologise.

Hinkel (*the smile vanishing*) My Minister? Apologise? To a Jew who signed a letter of protest?

Strauss What letter of protest?

Hinkel You didn't know? A letter signed by among others Thomas Mann and this Jew Stefan Zweig protesting against the list we drew up of cultural leaders opposed to the Führer. The Germans who signed we deprived of German citizenship. Well, they are after all despoilers of our culture. And I think it rather impertinent for an Austrian Jew to sign a letter of protest about what happens in Germany, don't you? There will, of course, be a price to pay. (*Hesitates, then with care.*) But, that's not – there is another –

He falls silent.

Pauline (*a slow realisation*) You did not come here because my husband invited you. You have other things to say.

45

Hinkel hesitates again.

Hinkel (*to Pauline*) I would greatly appreciate it, dear lady, if you would allow your esteemed husband and I to talk alone. I have to deliver a private message from Dr Goebbels –

Strauss I'd like my wife to stay.

Hinkel (*icy, brusque*) Then perhaps you would prefer to come and see my Minister in Berlin. In person.

A charged silence. Pauline sweeps from the room. Silence.

Strauss Well?

Hinkel This is a delicate matter. (*The smile.*) Dr Goebbels has asked me to alert you to an order that is about to be issued to all theatres in Germany.

Strauss What order?

Hinkel No works by Jews are to be produced. Or even those works in which a Jew has participated.

Strauss (*taken aback*) Does that mean – does that include my work?

Hinkel Only your work in which you have collaborated with a Jew.

Strauss Zweig.

Hinkel Yes. And von Hofmannsthal.

Strauss Von Hofmannsthal?

Hinkel He was a quarter-Jew, was he not? We make no distinctions.

Strauss explodes.

Strauss This is contemptible. I will protest to the highest authorities. I will appeal to the Führer himself. I am not going to obey this order. And you may tell that to Dr Goebbels. And if you won't, I will. If necessary in Berlin. In person.

Silence. Eventually, Hinkel smiles as if he is changing the subject.

Hinkel Have you heard or read about the problems we are having with Wilhelm Furtwängler?

Strauss No.

Hinkel Furtwängler hires too many Jew artists for his opera performances. He champions Paul Hindemith, a standard-bearer of decadence. Hindemith is German, of course, but you have only to listen to his music to possess the most drastic proof of how strongly the Jew infection has taken hold of our national body. Furthermore, Furtwängler writes letters of complaint to the press and has a Jew secretary. To crown it all Goering has made him a Prussian Privy Councillor. It's not to my Minister's liking.

Strauss So? What has all this to do with the performances of my operas?

Hinkel (*ignoring the question*) We will have to find a way to make him toe the line. Not easy. The Führer, alas, is his greatest admirer. But I have taken it upon myself to see that the position of his Jew secretary is made untenable – (*Breaks off.*) But in your case –

He falls silent, smiling.

Strauss (*on edge*) What do you mean, 'in my case'? I have said time and time again that I greatly admire Adolf Hitler, but I will not toe the line under any circumstances.

47

I composed music under the Kaiser and during the Weimar Republic. Music is indifferent to regimes. My new opera, *The Silent Woman*, libretto by Stefan Zweig, is almost ready to be staged and I tell you now, it will be staged.

Hinkel continues to smile.

Hinkel My Minister asked me to convey his enormous admiration for all your great achievements. He has no doubt that you are the finest example of what is best in German music.

Strauss Thank you, but I am not looking for good reviews at the moment. I am looking for my operas to be performed.

Hinkel My Minister urges you to co-operate with us. Because in your case he believes that opposition would be more dangerous.

Strauss (*exasperated*) More dangerous than what, more dangerous for whom? I don't understand what you mean by 'in your case'. What is so special about my case?

Silence.

Hinkel (*steel*) Your daughter-in-law is a Jew, am I right?

Strauss freezes.

Your grandchildren are therefore also Jews. Half-Jews.

Silence.

Dr Goebbels wanted me to make it clear that you are very important to us. He urges you to support our endeavours to cleanse German music from degenerate influences. If you do, you have his word that no harm will come to any member of your family. I'm sure you understand now. I'll be perfectly frank. We need you. To that end, I have the honour to inform you that my

Minister invites you to become President of the Reich Chamber of Music.

Silence.

I will take your silence as acceptance.

No response.

Furtwängler is to be your deputy.

No response.

And I should drop this matter about the Jew Zweig. Or, rather, the Jews Zweig. (*He chuckles.*) I can't see my Minister being helpful in any way.

Silence.

I won't keep you. It's been such a great honour for me to meet you. Please make my farewells to your delightful wife. (*His broad grin.*) President of the Reich Chamber of Music, I bid you farewell. (*Gives the Nazi salute.*) Heil Hitler!

> *He goes.*
> *Strauss is perfectly still, staring into space, appalled. After a moment, Pauline re-enters and immediately sees his distress.*

Pauline What is it? What did he say? What was the message?

Strauss (*barely audible*) I am to be President of the Reich Chamber of Music.

Pauline But that will mean working for them –

Strauss I couldn't refuse. I must do as I'm told.

Pauline Why, why do as you're told?

Strauss Or else.

Pauline (*desperate*) Or else what?

He breaks down.

Strauss Alice. The grandchildren. They'll be protected if –

Pauline puts a hand to cover her mouth to stifle a cry.

I had no choice.

He struggles for control.

Zweig's villa, Salzburg, August 1934.
Zweig, in his shirtsleeves, staring into space. After a moment, Lotte enters.

Lotte Dr Strauss is here. I've offered him refreshment but he declined. He's washing his hands. He seems very agitated. Or elated. I can't tell which.

Zweig Is his wife with him?

Lotte No, thank heavens, she terrifies me.

Zweig She means well.

Lotte Are you sure?

Zweig (*a smile*) Show him in.

Lotte goes. Zweig puts on his jacket as Strauss enters, greatly excited.

Strauss My dear Zweig –

Zweig Dear Doctor.

Strauss (*gleeful*) I cannot wait to tell you the latest developments.

Zweig Good or bad?

Strauss Last week, I was conducting in Bayreuth. Talk about fanatics, the Wagners want Hitler investigated to make sure he's a Nazi.

Zweig smiles.

I conducted *Parsifal*. Toscanini refused to conduct there on political grounds and I substituted for him. I did so, believe me, to save Bayreuth. Anyway, Goebbels also happened to be present and he paid me a private visit.

Zweig What did he want?

Strauss They won't allow me to have a Jewish librettist. They will not allow *The Silent Woman* to be performed.

Zweig (*quiet, distressed*) Oh my God –

Strauss No, no, listen, I told him I had no wish to make difficulties for him or for the Führer and that I was quite willing to withdraw *The Silent Woman* but I said that would result in a horrible scandal for the Third Reich. I kept a perfectly straight face, you'd have been proud of me. He became evasive and I thought incoherent. He said, 'I can muzzle the press but I can't guarantee that somebody won't throw a stink bomb during the premiere.' God knows what he meant. And then guess what he suggested?

Zweig Tell me –

Strauss That we submit the text to Hitler himself.

He chuckles.

Zweig Hitler's going to read the libretto?

Strauss No, no, he's read it, or had someone read it. Goebbels said if Hitler found nothing objectionable, then permission would be given for the premiere. And you know what? Whether he actually read it or not I have no idea, but nothing objectionable was found and, please prepare yourself for this – (*Triumph.*) – permission has been given.

Zweig forces a smile.

So, *bravi, bravi*, absolutely excellent as they say in *Cosi fan tutte*! (*He laughs.*) And do you know why Hitler gave permission?

Zweig No, why?

Strauss He was terrified that if he said no, my wife would pay him a visit. (*He chuckles.*) Little Goebbels didn't know what hit him. I said, 'Are you going to ban Mozart because his librettist, Lorenzo da Ponte, was a Jew?' 'We will have the texts rewritten,' he said, becoming very flustered and added, 'We're certainly banning Bizet because Halévi was a Jew. *Carmen* is the most obscene of operas.' I said, 'That's idiotic,' and then told him about a questionnaire I received asking if I was an Aryan artist and to give the names of two witnesses who could vouch for my ability in my chosen profession. I wrote in Mozart and Richard Wagner. He was reeling. I also told him that I intended to collaborate with you on all my future operatic projects because you were indispensable to me. He said I would have to submit the subjects for approval. I waved that aside. (*Beaming.*) So. The world premiere of *The Silent Woman* will be on the 24th of June in Dresden, in one of the most beautiful opera houses in all Germany. Hitler himself is to attend. And so will little Goebbels.

Zweig Will you conduct?

Strauss No, no, it's always dangerous to conduct a first performance of one's own work. No, von Schuch is doing it. He's not exactly Wilhelm Furtwängler, but perfectly competent.

Zweig I wish I could be there.

Strauss (*aghast*) What do you mean? But you must be there. I insist. You have to attend rehearsals, make changes if necessary, but above all enjoy the work you have helped to create.

No response.

You must be there.

Zweig With Hitler in the box? No, I'll be honest with you, I don't want to go to Germany at this time. I'm not afraid. But I don't want it said that I was surrendering to those in power to achieve God knows what. You know how the press would distort it. I don't want to feed the journalists' imagination in any way whatsoever.

Brief silence.

Strauss I understand. And in my heart, I agree with you.

Brief silence.

And don't you think it's a sad time when an artist of my rank has to ask a runt of a minister what he may or may not set to music and what he may or may not have performed?

Zweig Yes, I think it's a sad time.

Strauss But Zweig, you realise what a triumph this is for both of us. We have beaten them. So, start thinking of another subject for me to work on. Before the premiere. We must strike while the iron is sizzling.

Zweig I'm going abroad shortly –

Strauss I'll visit you anywhere of your choosing. We must have something to work on before the premiere, it's vital.

Silence.

Zweig My dear friend, you won't like what I'm about to say. We're cursed to live in the world as it is now. And the world as it is now has made it clear that our future collaboration is no longer possible.

Strauss is appalled.

Strauss But that just isn't true, quite the contrary –

Zweig Things are going to get worse, not better. We have to dismiss from our thoughts any notion of security. You must work with other librettists.

Strauss You can't mean that –

Zweig I will try to find subjects that may interest you but it's not possible for me to write them.

Strauss I won't have anyone else.

Zweig turns on him.

Zweig (*trembling, desperate*) How can I make you understand? How can I make you face reality?

Strauss (*angry*) My reality is composing music, that's what I do, that's what I've done all my life.

Zweig I don't want to be harsh, but are you sure it's not your hiding place? Isn't that your escape when the world becomes unbearable?

Strauss It's my way of life. If I don't write music, I die. You, you of all people, should understand. It's not as if you were a bank manager or a shopkeeper. Try telling a layman that your life depends on clutching at sounds in your head and translating them into hieroglyphics on

54

a page. Try telling them that without it you are deprived of oxygen, of your blood supply, of life itself. Most men of my age are retired, tending their gardens, or trying to stuff sailing boats into wine bottles. I swear to you that if I stop, I drop.

Zweig No one understands or admires your creativity more than I, your energy, your lust to compose, but it's for those very reasons that I have to distance myself from you –

Strauss No, no, I won't have it –

Zweig Not for my safety, but for yours. I don't believe you fully realise the danger.

Strauss To hell with the danger! I will not give you up because it so happens that we now have an anti-Semitic government. By their own admission they need me. I play along with them for one reason and one reason only, so that I can go on composing. And I can only go on composing if you provide me with libretti. We will get away with it.

Zweig We won't. They will destroy you. (*Pointedly.*) And your family.

Silence. Strauss fights tears.

Strauss Don't abandon me. Don't bury me in sand.

Zweig I will do my best to find subjects for you. And I will make a list of other librettists.

Strauss I don't want to hear about other librettists. I don't – (*Stops as an idea strikes him; becomes excited.*) Wait a moment, wait a moment, how about this? If you do find a subject for me, you will write it, but let us agree that no one will ever know about it or about my setting it to music. Once the score is finished, it will go into a safe

55

that will be opened only when we both consider the time propitious. Will you at least do that for me? (*Deeply felt.*) All I want in life is to be allowed to compose.

Silence.

Zweig You know I'm devoted to you and that gives me licence to be frank and honest with you. (*Gathering himself.*) Sometimes I have the feeling that you're not quite aware – and this is to your credit – that you're not aware of your historical importance, of your – your greatness. You think too modestly about yourself. Everything you do is destined to be of significance. One day, your letters, your decisions, will be meat and drink to historians. You will belong to all mankind, like Wagner and Brahms. And that's precisely why it's not right that your art should ever be practised in secret. Even if neither of us ever mentioned that I'd written something for you, it would inevitably come out. Inevitably. It's beneath you. You have earned the right to exercise your art in public, not to seek refuge in secrecy. And if I wrote for you publicly it would be considered a provocation. So. Please agree to what I now say. I will be happy to advise anybody who might work for you, to sketch things out for him, without compensation, without boasting about it, simply for the pleasure of serving you and your music. I will co-operate with anyone you care to name, without credit or reward.

Silence.

Strauss You make me weep, but please, please stay with me. Don't turn me into an ailing, unemployed old-aged pensioner. And who could write a usable libretto for me even if you were to co-operate generously and unselfishly? I told Goebbels over and over again that I searched for librettists for fifty years. Dozens of texts were sent to me.

To find *Salome* was sheer luck, although I don't believe in luck. It was in truth the forked stick inside me. *Elektra* introduced me to von Hofmannsthal. We rose to heaven, *Der Rosenkavalier, Ariadne* – (*Breaks off.*) After his death, I thought I would never write again. Then you.

Zweig (*a sad smile*) I was, perhaps, your piece of bad luck.

Strauss You are not to think like that. (*Pleading.*) Listen to me, listen to me, I am absolutely confident that they won't put any obstacles in the way of a second Zweig opera. I will never find another writer of your brilliance. Let's go on working but keep it confidential. That isn't undignified, it's wise.

Zweig (*steel*) It's madness. It's immoral.

Silence.

Strauss You were frank with me. I'll return the compliment. I don't believe you. I don't believe that you are acting entirely out of consideration for me. You know what I think? I think that by refusing to collaborate with me, you are indulging in a gesture, showing support for your fellow Jews, am I right? In times of persecution, isn't that what Jews have always done? Banded together?

Silence.

Zweig I have never been much of a Jew. Nevertheless, that's what I am, whether by blood or tradition I know not, but that's what I am. Gustav Mahler was fond of saying, 'An artist who is a Jew is like a swimmer with one short arm – he has to swim twice as hard to reach the shore.' But I've never felt that. I've always regarded myself as an Austrian and a European. And that, I believe, is how I've been perceived. Yet now, the world I knew – the world I was born into, the world of yesterday– is ended. The culture which was my religion has been blasphemed. They have made of me a heretic. I accept the role. When I look into the future I see nothing but death and putrefaction. So I say with Cymbeline, 'Let us meet the time as it seeks us.' I have no choice but to be what I am.

Silence.

Hotel Belvedere, Dresden, June 1935.
Light on Pauline playing patience. Strauss joins her, lighting a cigar. He is nervous.

Strauss Where is that man?

Pauline Not here, obviously.

Strauss How far is it from this hotel to the opera house?

No response.

I could do it in five minutes, he's been gone for half an hour.

Pauline It was a good dress rehearsal yesterday.

Strauss (*flaring*) The dress rehearsal isn't the performance. Where is he? I send him on a simple errand and he takes an hour.

Pauline Half an hour.

Strauss Don't be so irritating – can't you see I'm nervous? How do people like him get these jobs?

Pauline His job is intendant not errand boy.

Strauss Well then, things have come to a pretty pass when an intendant –

Paul Adolph, aged sixty-six, enters, with a rolled-up poster under his arm. He is very upset.

Strauss And about time –

Adolph Dreadful news.

Pauline *and* **Strauss** What?

Adolph The Führer is unable to be present tonight.

Strauss Why?

Adolph A thunderstorm has made it impossible for his aeroplane to leave Hamburg.

Pauline What about Goebbels?

Adolph The same, they're together, neither of them will attend.

Strauss Do you think it's true?

Adolph Do I think what's true?

Strauss That there's a thunderstorm in Hamburg. Or is he just finding an excuse not to attend?

Adolph Well, I hadn't thought. I'm sure it's true, why should the Führer lie? I'm so dreadfully disappointed.

Pauline Not me.

Strauss Pauline –

Pauline It's bad enough having a world premiere. The last thing one needs is the government in attendance.

Adolph (*to Strauss*) But you will sit in the box just the same?

Strauss I may, I may not. I may pace, I may walk the streets, I haven't decided.

Pauline My husband will sit in the box.

Adolph And you, too, dear lady –

Strauss Well, of course, if I'm in the box, she'll be in the box.

Adolph Such a shame about the Führer. Everyone was so excited.

Strauss Everyone except my wife. Have you brought the poster?

Adolph I've looked at it, it's perfectly in order – (*A joke.*) Your name is spelt correctly –

He unrolls the poster. He holds it up for Strauss to read. Strauss studies it carefully. He becomes profoundly angry.

Strauss (*seething, very slowly*) Where is the name of Stefan Zweig?

Adolph (*alarmed*) What?

Strauss I asked you a question. Where is the name of my librettist, Stefan Zweig?

No response; Pauline comes to Strauss's side and also reads.

The only credit I can see is 'Adapted from the English of Ben Jonson'. It doesn't say by whom.

Adolph We couldn't do otherwise. Surely you understand the reasons –

Strauss Is it the same on the programme?

Adolph Of course –

Strauss What do you intend to do about it?

Adolph I am not sure I can do anything about it –

Strauss (*exploding*) Do or don't do what you like, but I am leaving. Now. The performance will have to take place without me.

Pauline Sweetheart, please –

Adolph But the world's press –

Strauss Have I made myself clear? I insist that the name of Stefan Zweig appears in all relevant material. Have stickers printed immediately. Otherwise, I will create such a scandal –

Adolph I – I –

Strauss finds a pen, grabs the poster, and writes on it.

Strauss In all relevant material. The same size as mine. 'Libretto by Stefan Zweig.'

He thrusts the poster into Adolph's hands. Silence.

Adolph I hope you realise what you're asking of me.

Strauss I realise what I'm asking of you.

No one moves. A long silence.

Adolph Very well. It will be done.

He goes.

Pauline (*quiet*) Admirable. But I pray that we are the only ones you've put at risk.

Zweig villa, Salzburg, June 1935.
    Dim light on Zweig alone. He is listening to a broadcast performance of The Silent Woman. *The reception is bad, persistent atmospherics, hissing, whistling.*

After a moment, he weeps silently. His whole body shudders. His face contorts as he tries to control his pain. The music and the atmospherics continue.

Zweig villa, Salzburg, and Hotel Belvedere, Dresden, June 1935.
The telephone ringing in darkness. Light as Zweig enters and answers it.

Zweig Stefan Zweig.

Light on Strauss and Pauline in the Belvedere.

Strauss Zweig, my dear friend, a triumph, a great triumph. Did you hear it?

Zweig I – I – listened –

Lotte, dressed for travelling, enters.

Strauss Well? Well? What did you think?

No response.

Are you there, Zweig?

Zweig Yes, I'm here –

Strauss What was your opinion of the opera? Were you pleased?

Zweig The reception wasn't perfect –

Strauss Nonsense, we had a standing ovation. A packed house, a superb performance and splendid reviews!

Zweig Excellent. (*Covering the mouthpiece, to Lotte.*) Strauss. A great success last night –

Strauss I'm pleased you were able to hear it because they said they were going to jam the broadcast. Now. I have to get back to Garmisch so I'll miss the second performance but it's also almost sold out. I will keep you informed. So, Zweig, where is my next libretto?

Zweig We'll be in touch –

Strauss Think of something, soon –

Zweig Goodbye –

Strauss Don't let me down –

> *They replace the receivers. Lights out on Strauss and Pauline.*
> *Zweig is still, troubled.*

Lotte It went well?

Zweig Apparently.

Lotte I've put our suitcases in the hall. The taxi should be here at any moment. (*Sensing his preoccupation.*) Stefan, what is it?

Zweig He inhabits a castle of dreams. He's rejoicing over matters remote from reality, while somewhere in the invisible are persons we've never known or seen, making decisions about our lives and every other life in Europe. But Richard Strauss is bubbling with success and begging me for a new libretto.

Lotte But you're pleased, too, aren't you? You must be –

Zweig It's an illusion. It's irrelevant. He behaves as if everything is normal, as if music and the theatre were as they always were, central to our lives, while out in the void there are men who permit freedom or compel slavery, who destroy us or spare us, who determine peace or war. And here we are, like everybody else, defenceless as flies, helpless as snails, waiting, staring into black night, doomed, while life and death, our innermost beings and our future are in hazard. And Strauss is quite oblivious.

Silence.

Lotte (*tentative*) If you want to change your mind, if you want to stay and face whatever is in store, please know I want to stay with you. I will always do whatever you want to do.

Zweig Thank you, dearest, dearest Lotte, but the course is set.

Silence. Lotte smiles.

Lotte There's nothing for it then. We will become wandering Jews. That's no bad thing, is it? It's a perfectly honourable tradition.

He laughs. The sound of a car hooter, insistent.

Zweig (*a smile*) Very well, then. Let the wandering begin.

Strauss villa, Garmisch, 1935.
   Light on Hinkel, not smiling, facing Strauss and Pauline, seated, both tense.

Hinkel My Minister has asked me to put before you matters that have caused him great disquiet.

Pauline Now what?

Hinkel shoots her an icy glance.

Hinkel Dr Strauss, a letter that we believe was written by you has come into the hands of the Gestapo and forwarded to my Minister.

Pauline (*outraged*) Do you mean it was intercepted and read without my husband's –?

Hinkel (*turning on her*) Madam, I am here on behalf of Dr Josef Goebbels. Allow me to give you some advice. Keep your mouth tightly shut!

Pauline rises.

Pauline Don't you dare speak to me like that –

Strauss Pauline –

Pauline No, no, no, I won't have it. You may think yourself very important and powerful, Herr Hinkel, but let me remind you that you are an uninvited guest in my house –

Hinkel (*fighting for control*) Madam, I will tell you again –

Pauline And I will tell you that I demand you behave in a civilised way. How dare you talk to me like that? Where are your manners? We are not criminals. If you are intent on bullying and browbeating us, lock us in a cell and do your damnedest. But while you are in my house you will behave like a gentleman or leave. And you may tell that to your Minister. Have I made myself clear?

Hinkel, with enormous effort, controls himself, turns his back on her and faces Strauss. Pauline sits.
Hinkel takes out a small black notebook and a propelling pencil.

Hinkel The Jew Zweig has been under surveillance. He is, as you well know, in England, accompanied by his secretary, Fräulein Charlotte Altmann, a Jewess – not his wife, but they share a bedroom. (*The faintest of smiles.*) Our agent attended a reception at the Austrian Embassy at which they and other Jews were present. He says of her – (*Consults the notebook.*) 'You would forget that she was there. She remained almost non-existent.' (*Looks up.*) An ideal personality for a spy. Do you know if she is a spy?

Pauline A spy? What absolute nonsense. She is a young woman of character, of modest character. That may be unusual but it's not sinister. She is the very best type of –

She stops herself. Hinkel waits, as if he expects more. Then:

Hinkel No, they have not been engaged in overt political activity as far as we can ascertain. But perhaps you have other information that may be of help to us. Do you know, for example, if it is true that he has assigned his royalties from *The Silent Woman* to the Jewish Emergency Fund?

Strauss I am sure not.

Hinkel Why are you sure?

Strauss Because I would have known about it. Our royalties are dealt with jointly and I would have known. You mentioned a letter, what letter?

Hinkel (*producing a letter*) Was this written by you to the Jew Zweig presently resident in England, in the city of Bath?

He hands Strauss the letter. Strauss glances at it and stiffens, becoming alarmed.

Strauss Yes, but – but I can't see –

Hinkel Certain passages are underlined in blue pencil. Read them out and I will question you regarding their meaning and import.

Strauss (*flustered*) But – but you must understand the context, I was hoping to persuade him to change his mind, I wanted him to go on writing for me –

Hinkel Just read the passages, please.

Silence. Strauss steels himself.

Strauss (*hesitant, nervous*) 'Your Jewish obstinacy! Enough to make an anti-Semite of a man.'

Hinkel What did you mean by that?

Strauss Exactly what it says. Zweig was continuing to resist further collaborating with me and I was trying –

Hinkel But you say 'enough to make an anti-Semite of a man'. Does that mean you are not an anti-Semite, and if not, why not?

Strauss is bemused.

Strauss But that – that's like asking me why I'm not a coal miner or a ballet dancer? Because I'm not, that's why.

Hinkel Please take care with your replies, this is not a subject for a comic opera. (*Making a note.*) 'Not an anti-Semite.' (*Looks up.*) Continue.

Strauss (*reading*) 'Do you believe I am guided by the thought that I am German? Do you believe that Mozart composed as an "Aryan"? I know only two types of people: those with and those without talent. People exist for me only when they become an audience. Whether they are Chinese, Bavarians, New Zealanders or Berliners leaves me cold. What matters is that they pay the full price of admission –'

Hinkel Stop there. Are those really your sentiments?

Pauline My husband wouldn't have written them if they weren't.

Hinkel (*ignoring her*) Dr Strauss?

Strauss Yes. They are my sentiments.

Hinkel (*makes a note*) You realise the implications?

No response.

You espouse views entirely contrary to the ideals and policies of National Socialism.

Strauss I was merely trying to – to argue my case.

Hinkel Continue.

Strauss (*reading*) 'I urgently ask you to work on a libretto and to keep the matter secret –'

Hinkel By urging secrecy, you were deliberately conspiring to defy the Führer's edict that collaboration with a Jew is forbidden. Am I right?

No response. Hinkel makes a note.

Yes, next.

Strauss (*reading*) 'I am play-acting when I speak or appear as President of the Reich Chamber of Music. I do that only for good purposes and to prevent greater disasters. I would have accepted this troublesome honorary office under any government, but neither Kaiser Wilhelm nor Weimar offered it to me –'

Hinkel 'Play-acting'?

No response.

You have insulted my Minister, German culture and, worst of all, the Führer himself.

Strauss I meant no insult.

Pauline Can't you understand that my husband was in an ill humour with Zweig and wrote without any thought –?

68

Hinkel (*cutting her off*) Dr Strauss, you have
demonstrated serious shortcomings. My Minister requires
that you resign immediately as President of the Reich
Chamber of Music. You will do so by writing a letter to
the Führer himself. You will explain what you mean by
these offending passages in general, and why you pursue
the Jew Zweig in particular. You will further explain
why you visited Zweig in Salzburg when such visits were
forbidden. And my Minister will read the letter before
it is sent so that he can be certain you express sufficient
humility. (*Puts away his notebook and pencil.*) You
should know that the Intendant of the Dresden Opera
House, Paul Adolph, has been dismissed from his post
for allowing the name of the Jew Zweig to appear on the
posters and in the programme. I am further instructed
to inform you that, despite the favourable reviews of the
critics, there will be no more performances of *The Silent
Woman.* (*Now he smiles.*) One last thing. You will accept
a commission to write the Hymn for the Berlin Olympic
Games next year. (*To Pauline.*) I take it, madam, you
have nothing further to add to this conversation. (*Gives
the Nazi salute.*) Heil Hitler!

He marches out. Strauss and Pauline are silent, still.

Petropolis, Brazil, February 1942.
The distant sound of the samba, and carnival noise.
*Lotte, seated. She is strained and tense, staring into
space, playing in her hands with a small glass phial.*
*Zweig enters, carrying a single sheet of paper. He offers
it to her. She shakes her head. After a moment, he reads
from it.*

Zweig 'Before my wife, Charlotte, and I depart this life –'

Lotte No, no, no, no, no, no –

Zweig What?

Lotte Not me, leave my name out.

Zweig But we agreed –

Lotte We did not agree. It's you. It's your declaration, you are the important one –

Zweig Don't be ridiculous, Lotte, it's not a question of importance, we do this together –

Lotte We do. We will. But it is you alone who must speak. This is not a time for sentimentality. We must be scrupulously honest. You must not include me. I am a footnote –

Zweig Don't say such things –

Lotte Please.

Silence. With a pencil he makes some corrections. He reads:

Zweig 'Before I depart this life of my own free will and in my right mind, I want urgently to fulfil one last duty: I want to give thanks to this wonderful country of Brazil which afforded me such kindness and hospitality. Nowhere would we – would I have more gladly rebuilt my life, now that my native tongue is denied me, and Europe, my spiritual home, is destroying itself. But I am past sixty, and one would need superhuman powers to begin afresh. My powers have been exhausted by long years of homeless wandering. It seems to me, therefore, better to put an end now, without humiliation, to a life in which intellectual and artistic pursuits have been my joy, and personal freedom earth's most precious possession. I salute all my friends. May they live to see the dawn after the long night is over. We – I, all too impatient, am going on before. Stefan Zweig and – (*Breaks off.*) Stefan Zweig. Petropolis, 22nd of February 1942.'

Silence. He makes a few more corrections.

Lotte Good.

Zweig I wanted to explain that we would be unable to exist severed from Europe. But I couldn't find the words. In the end I decided to avoid the melodrama of suicide notes. It seemed best to keep it as simple as possible.

Lotte Yes. (*She rises.*) Shall I type a fair copy?

Zweig No. Thank you. I'll write it out again. It's best in my own hand.

Silence. She rises, holding the phial.

Lotte Don't be long.

Zweig No.

Lotte (*gazing at the phial*) And then –

She falls silent. He suddenly smiles at a memory.

Zweig 'And then I shall be wiser than you, My Lord Archbishop.'

Lotte (*baffled*) What?

Still smiling, he shakes his head. She exits. His smile fades and after a moment he follows her.

Garmisch, April 1945.
  Sounds of war. Machine-gun fire, explosions, orders shouted. Strauss, now aged eighty-one, in a state of great alarm, hands raised as if surrendering.

Strauss Don't shoot! Don't shoot! I am the composer of *Rosenkavalier*! Don't shoot! Leave me alone! I am the composer of *Rosenkavalier*!

  Pauline, now aged eighty-two, enters, grabs his arm.

Pauline Come away –

  She starts to lead him away.

American Soldier's Voice (*calling*) Say, Richard!

  They stop, look back.

Can we have your autograph?

Pauline If you want my husband's signature, come round to the back of the house. And don't forget to wipe your boots!

  They hurry away.

Munich, 1948.
  A pool of light on two chairs. Strauss and Pauline enter. He sits.

Strauss Would it be possible for my wife to sit beside me? My memory isn't what it was and I want to be sure I don't forget what may prove to be important.

  Pauline sits. Strauss consults notes.

I would like to say from the outset that I heartily welcome
my appearance before this Denazification Board. In
my humble opinion, it comes not a moment too soon.
Since the end of the war I have attended many premieres
of my work all over Europe, and was even invited to
England to partake in the revitalised Strauss Festival in
London, where I shared the podium with Sir Thomas
Beecham. It's time I believe that my own country
removed the stigma that clings to my name. (*Consults
notes.*) I have never belonged to any political party,
neither of the right nor the left. My party is art, only art.
You ask me to justify my activities during the particular
period in question. Yes, yes, I welcomed Hitler with high
hopes. Yes, I met all the leading Nazis on many occasions,
I kept in with them, I allowed myself to be courted by
them, I thought I could use them but they used me. Then
they discarded me when they realised I wasn't one of
them. I had to write an Olympic Hymn for them, and
music for the Japanese royal family, I was reduced to
composing kitsch –

He fights for control. Pauline whispers to him.

Yes, yes. You must understand that if ever I appeared to
collaborate with the Nazis it was because I did my utmost
to protect my Jewish daughter-in-law, Alice, and our
grandchildren. To some extent, I succeeded, though
several members of her family, including her mother, were
slaughtered. I even went to the gates of the concentration
camp in the hope of getting the old lady released. I told
them who I was, but the answer came, 'No access for
anybody.' No access – (*Breaks off.*) Alice herself was
humiliated, became ill, was not even permitted to attend
performances of my operas. But she and the children
survived. Survived. Thank God. (*Controls tears.*) What
would you have done in my shoes? Consigned them to

the gas chambers? I was compelled to protect my family. For that I feel no shame. My motives may not have been pure, but at least they were human. (*Gains control of himself.*) I've written little since the war. I'm considered old-fashioned. Well, I may not be a first-rate composer, but I am a first-class second-rate composer. (*He tries to smile.*) I'll go on, of course. I will never again write an opera, but now I am composing songs for soprano and orchestra –

He breaks off as one of his 'Four Last Songs' begins to be heard. He is lost for a moment. Pauline prompts him.

Pauline Zweig.

Strauss Yes. Also in my defence, although I find it humiliating to justify myself in this way, I should like to draw your attention to my collaboration with my Jewish colleague, Stefan Zweig. When I heard of his suicide in Brazil – (*He breaks down.*) What a terrible, terrible tragedy. A man of his genius. How could he do such a thing? He had rare and wondrous gifts. He was the most admirable of human beings. If we are to have a better world he should have been one of its creators. Men of his integrity are to be numbered – (*Breaks off.*) I – I loved that man. (*Fights for control.*) To take poison was the most vile betrayal. Why, why, why? He abhorred violence and wasn't it violence to take his own life? And his wife, a shy, devoted – (*Suddenly fierce.*) You accuse me of being a collaborator but what about Zweig?

Pauline No, no, sweetheart, don't –

Strauss You think they didn't want to add another Jew to the millions they murdered? Of course they wanted him dead. And he obliged. He did their bidding. Yes, he was the –

He sobs. Pauline does her best to comfort him. His music continues.

The End.

TAKING SIDES

For Bernard Levin

Author's Note

Wilhelm Furtwängler (1886–1954) was the outstanding conductor of his generation, rivalled only by Arturo Toscanini. He was at the height of his powers when Adolf Hitler became Chancellor of Germany in 1933. Many of his colleagues, because they were Jews, were forced to leave; others, non-Jews, opponents of the regime, chose exile as an act of protest. Furtwangler decided to stay; as a result he was accused of serving Nazism. This was and still is the principal accusation made against him.

He came before a Denazification Tribunal in Berlin in 1946 which was conducted by his fellow Germans who questioned him for two days. He was cleared of all charges but was never able to cleanse himself entirely of the Nazi stench that still clings to his memory.

The Tribunal's evidence had been prepared in the first instance by the British, then taken over, apparently, by two groups of Americans: one, in Wiesbaden, which assisted Furtwängler with his defence; the other, in Berlin, which was responsible for building the case against him.

Little or nothing is known of the motives and methods of this second group which is the focus of *Taking Sides*. What is undeniable, however, is that Furtwängler was humiliated, relentlessly pursued and, after his acquittal, disinformation concerning him appeared in American newspapers. This may or may not have been justified. It all depends on the side you take.

Taking Sides was first performed at the Minerva Theatre, Chichester, on 18 May 1995, and this production transferred to the Criterion Theatre, London, on 3 July 1995, with the following cast:

Major Steve Arnold Michael Pennington
Emmi Straube Geno Lechner
Tamara Sachs Suzanne Bertish
Helmuth Rode Gawn Grainger
David Wills Christopher Simon
Wilhelm Furtwängler Daniel Massey

Directed by Harold Pinter
Lighting by Mick Hughes
Costumes by Tom Rand
Designer Eileen Diss

Under the title *Za I Przeciw*, the play was performed on the same day in Poland at the Teatr im. Juliusza Slowackiego W. Krakowie with the following cast:

Major Steve Arnold Marcin Kusminski
Emmi Straube Joanna Jankowska
Tamara Sachs Urszula Popiel
Helmuth Rode Mariusz Wojciechowski
Porucznik David Wills Marek Sawicki
Wilhelm Furtwängler Michal Pawlicki

Directed by Tomasz Zygadio
Translator Michal Ronikier
Designer Jerzy Rudski

Taking Sides was first first produced in the United States by Alexander Cohen at the Brooks Atkinson Theatre, New York, on 27 October 1996 with the following cast:

Major Steve Arnold Ed Harris
Emmi Straube Elizabeth Marvel
Tamara Sachs Ann Dowd
Helmuth Rode Norbert Weisser
David Wills Michael Stuhlbarg
Wilhelm Furtwängler Daniel Massey

Directed by David Jones
Lighting by Howell Binkley
Costumes by Theoni Aldredge
Scenic Designer David Jenkins

Taking Sides was revived at the Minerva Theatre, Chichester, in repertory with *Collaboration*, on 21 July 2008, with the following cast:

Major Steve Arnold David Horovitch
Emmi Straube Sophie Roberts
Tamara Sachs Melanie Jessop
Helmuth Rode Pip Donaghy
David Wills Martin Hutson
Wilhelm Furtwängler Michael Pennington

Director Philip Franks
Designer Simon Higlett
Design Assistant Gerry Bunzl
Lighting Designer Mark Jonathan
Sound Designer John A. Leonard
Composer Matthew Scott
Costumer Supervisor Bill Butler

Characters

Major Steve Arnold

Emmi Straube

Tamara Sachs

Helmuth Rode

Lieutenant David Wills

Wilhelm Furtwängler

The action takes place in Major Arnold's office
in the American Zone of occupied Berlin, 1946

Act One
February, morning

Act Two
Scene One: April, night
Scene Two: July, morning

Setting

Major Arnold's office is an island surrounded by the rubble
of a city flattened by Allied bombs. The room is in a
former government building. Not everyone visiting the
office need pass through the rubble. The office may also
be reached from unseen approaches. The room is barely
furnished but, incongruously, there is an ornate desk
which Arnold uses. His German secretary, Emmi Straube,
has a table, a typewriter and a field telephone. There are
two other smaller tables, one with a record player and
a pile of records, the other with an extension to the field
telephone.

Between Arnold's desk and Emmi's table stands a plain
upright chair which is for those being questioned. Nearer
Arnold's desk there is a rather more comfortable chair for
visitors. There is a door that leads to a waiting room.

In Act Two, central heating radiators are in place and the
telephone system has been streamlined.

Act One

*February. Just before nine a.m. Freezing cold. One
miserable wood-burning stove. All wear overcoats,
gloves, scarves. From the gramophone in Major Steven
Arnold's office comes the sound of the last minutes of the
final movement of Beethoven's Fifth Symphony, conducted
by Wilhelm Furtwängler. Arnold is asleep, his legs
stretched out on his desk. He could be any age, between
thirty-five and early fifties.*

*Emmi Straube is at her table listening to the music and
watching Arnold. She is in her early twenties, pale, almost
nondescript. In the bomb rubble, heavily wrapped up,
like a vagrant, sits Tamara Sachs, thirty-two, waiting.*

*Helmuth Rode, late forties, wearing threadbare clothes
and a balaclava, enters the bomb site. He starts rummaging
for anything he can find. Then he hears the music but
cannot identify its source.*

*Lieutenant David Wills, aged twenty-four, enters
purposefully through the bomb rubble. Rode scuttles
away. David passes and disappears around the back of
the office. Tamara barely glances at him.*

*The music continues. Arnold sleeps. Emmi listens and
watches. The office door opens and David reappears. He
sees Arnold asleep and retreats. After a moment, the
music ends and Emmi takes off the record.*

Emmi Major Arnold, the music has ended.

He doesn't stir.

Major Arnold?

He wakes with a start, as if from a bad dream.

The music has ended, Major.

He breathes more easily.

Arnold I wish you'd call me Steve, Emmi.

Emmi You fell asleep.

Arnold That's true, Emmi, I did.

Emmi It is very difficult for me to understand how you can fall asleep during Beethoven's Fifth Symphony.

Arnold Then I'll explain, Emmi. I fell asleep during Beethoven's Fifth Symphony because Beethoven's Fifth Symphony bores me shitless.

Emmi You are joking again. Are you joking? I am never sure when you are joking. I think you are always joking when you are being coarse.

Arnold No, Emmi, I am never joking when I'm being coarse.

Emmi I don't like it when you are coarse.

Arnold Then you must be having a really bad time of it, Emmi.

Emmi You should listen to Beethoven carefully, Major. My favourite is the Eighth Symphony. But you should listen especially to the Ninth. Beethoven wrote it in his last years. It is one of the most beautiful pieces of music ever written. You should listen to it, Major.

Arnold Is it the same length as Number Five? Or as he got older did he write shorter?

Emmi Yes, you are joking, but you must listen to it, Major. That's why I have brought these recordings so that you should know with whom you are dealing.

Arnold I know with whom I'm dealing. (*He goes to the stove, warms himself.*) I knew another band leader once. Name of Dix Dixon. Small time. Alto sax. Not bad. Not good, but not bad. Played one-night stands in Illinois and Michigan. A house he owned, where he and the band used to stay, burned down. Lost everything. Well, almost everything. But I got him. You know how? Because there's always one question the guilty can't answer. Get a sign writer, write it big: THERE'S ALWAYS ONE QUESTION THE GUILTY CAN'T ANSWER. In Dix's case, it was, 'How come, Dix, everybody lost everything except you? You've got your clothes, your sax, how come?' Couldn't answer. He was dumb. Boy, was he dumb. Owed the bookies. You understand, don't you, Emmi? He burned down his own house for the insurance money. We used to call that Jewish lightning.

He chuckles. No response from Emmi.

How many people do I have to see before the big boy's due?

Emmi (*consulting a file*) Just one. Helmuth Rode. Second violinist, 1935 to the present. Also, there is a request from Wiesbaden that you see a Mrs Tamara Sachs. I have talked to her on the telephone and she will be coming at two o'clock.

Arnold Anything from Wiesbaden's got to be bad news. What's this Mrs Sachs want?

Emmi She wouldn't say. Oh, and Major, a young officer put his head round the door a moment ago, saw that you were asleep and then disappeared.

Arnold Who was he?

Emmi I don't know. I have never seen him before. (*Consulting a message pad.*) And two other messages.

Captain Vernay may visit later. Colonel Volkov will not be attending.

Arnold That's a relief. Nothing from the British?

Emmi No.

Arnold Where's that young officer now?

Emmi I don't know, he came and went.

Arnold Go find him, will you, Emmi?

Emmi exits. Arnold adds wood to the heater. In the rubble, Rode reappears, crosses the bomb site, stops to pick up a cigarette butt and then hurries off towards the rear of Arnold's office and disappears. Tamara sits and waits. Emmi re-enters, holding the door for David, who comes to attention, salutes smartly.

David Lieutenant Wills reporting to Major Arnold. Sir.

Arnold For Chrissakes I hate that shit, cut it out. My name's Steve. What's yours?

David (*slightly disconcerted*) David. David Wills.

Arnold Who are you?

David I've taken over from Captain Greenwood. I'm your new liaison officer with Allied Intelligence.

Arnold What happened to Hank?

David Captain Greenwood was ordered to Nürnberg. Seems they need more interpreters at the trial.

Arnold So you're dealing with the British now.

David Yes, sir.

Arnold You call me 'sir' again, I'll make you listen to Beethoven.

David only half smiles.

You seen that Limey major yet, the one who talks like
he's got ice cubes in his mouth? I can't tell if he's speaking
German or English, what the hell's his name?

David Major Richards.

Arnold Yeah, Alan Richards.

David I talked to him this morning but he was just
rushing off to an urgent meeting.

Arnold An urgent meeting. Yeah, the Hinkel Archive.

David Yes.

Arnold Do you know what's in the Hinkel Archive?

David No.

Arnold And if it turns out to be important, you think the
British are going to share it with their allies?

David He said he'd call to let you know. He said he was
very disappointed. He wanted to be here today. Especially
today.

Arnold eyes him up and down.

Arnold We recruiting children now?

David (*a smile*) I guess so.

Arnold Where you from?

David I was born here.

Arnold smiles, waits, gives no help.

Not in Berlin. In Hamburg.

Still no help from Arnold.

I escaped in '34. When I was twelve. (*Pause.*) My parents sent me to my uncle in Philadelphia. They were to follow. But they delayed and delayed. They did not follow.

Nothing from Arnold.

Our family name is Weill. But that doesn't sound well in English. My uncle changed it to Wills.

Arnold Did you hear that, Emmi? David here was born in Hamburg.

Emmi Yes, I heard.

Arnold I'm sorry about your parents.

Uneasy pause.

Oh, this is Emmi Straube. She records the interviews. She's been with me a week. she's a good German, aren't you, Emmi? Her father was in the plot against Adolf. (*Pause.*) Well, what kind of an intelligence officer are you, David? You should have asked a question. You should have asked, 'But how do we know she didn't report her father for being in the plot against Adolf?' Isn't that what he should've asked, Emmi?

No response.

Emmi's okay. We've checked her out. You're okay, aren't you, Emmi?

Emmi Shall I see if Mr Rode is here? It's after nine.

Arnold When I say so, Emmi, when I say so. (*To David.*) I like to keep them waiting. Makes them sweat. Which is a kindness in this weather, wouldn't you say?

Emmi I expect Mr Rode's here, Major.

Arnold She won't call me Steve, David. She is so correct. And she likes books and poetry and she's just crazy for

94

Beethoven, aren't you, Emmi? Do you like Beethoven, David?

David Yes.

Arnold Yes. I thought you looked funny when I threatened you with the old bastard. And I guess you admire musicians.

David Some.

Arnold Don't.

David Don't what?

Arnold This is like a criminal investigation, David. Musicians, morticians, lawyers, butchers, doctors, clerks. They're all the same. I saw Bergen-Belsen two days after it was liberated. I know what I'm talking about. I've seen things with these eyes – do you know what I'm talking about, David?

David Yes.

Arnold Think of your parents. Don't think of musicians. We're after the big guy here, the band leader, that's the one we're going to nail. You know what I call him, David? I call him a piece of shit. I call 'em all pieces of shit.

David Captain Greenwood said hard evidence against him is difficult to come by.

Arnold Let's talk about it after we get through with this guy Rode. Here's how we do it. This is my show, I ask the questions. If you want to ask a question, raise a finger so he can't see. I'll signal yea or nay. Understood?

David Yes.

Arnold I'll explain my technique. I tell the shitheads why they're here. Then I only ever ask two questions. First, anything that comes to mind. 'How you feeling today?',

'Are you getting enough to eat?', 'You need some cigarettes?' Real friendly. Second, I say, 'I see from your questionnaire that you were never a member of the Party, is that right?' 'Absolutely right, I was never a member of the Party.' And then I wait. I say nothing. I wait. And then they talk. Oh, boy, do they talk. And they'll tell you what a great guy the band leader is, how he defied Adolf and Hermann and Josef. Oh yes, and they always get in the baton story.

David What's the baton story?

Arnold How many have I questioned, Emmi?

Emmi Twenty-eight.

Arnold So this guy –?

Emmi Helmuth Rode –

Arnold Rode, he'll be the twenty-ninth. You'll hear the baton story for the first time, I'm going to hear it for the twenty-ninth. Oh yeah, and they always manage to find out Emmi's last name, don't they, Emmi? 'Straube,' they say. 'Any relation to Joachim Straube?' 'My father,' Emmi says. 'A great man,' they say, 'a great hero.' You see, David, what they're trying to do is cover the band leader in roses in the hope they'll come up smelling just as sweet. But it's difficult to smell sweet after you've crawled through raw sewage. I was in insurance before the war, a claims assessor, what were you in?

David College.

Arnold And when all this is over?

David I'd like to teach history.

Arnold History. You need a good memory for history, don't you? All those dates and battles. Your memory good?

David Not bad –

Arnold Me, I've got a terrific memory. I've been examined by psychologists. Because of my memory, nothing else. I've got what they call 'total recall'. I remember everything. It's a curse. (*Suddenly, as if briefly invaded by a memory which he shakes off.*) Yeah, a curse, believe me. But I'm bad at names. It's what the shrinks call 'selective'. Tell you the truth, my recall's not total, but it's pretty good. Yeah, insurance. I was trained by a guy called Lou O'Donnell, a kind of Jimmy Cagney type. Pushy, smart, persistent – boy, was that guy persistent. Lou taught me to look out for what he called 'repetitive evidence', because ninety-nine times out of a hundred it covers a conspiracy to defraud. You think a whole orchestra, what, a hundred and twenty or so guys, could be orchestrated?

David I don't know, I guess it's possible –

Arnold Yeah, me too, I guess it's possible. Okay, Emmi, let's get Mr Rode in.

Emmi exits.

You sit there.

David sits and Arnold goes to his desk.

Remember, I do the talking. Just the two questions, then we wait. You'll see.

Emmi re-enters.

Emmi Mr Helmuth Rode.

Rode enters, removes his balaclava, bows to Arnold and David. Emmi sits at her table and takes notes. Rode glances nervously round, twists his neck to read the record labels.

Arnold Sit down, Helmuth.

Rode sits. Arnold consults a file.

I want you to understand why you're here. This is a
preliminary investigation into Wilhelm Furtwängler,
former Prussian Privy Councillor, who is banned from
public life under Control Council Directive No. 24 and
who's applied to come before the Tribunal of Artists of the
Denazification Commission. We're interested in what he
was up to from 1933 to the end of the war, understood?

Rode Yes.

Arnold I have your questionnaire here. (*Reading.*) Helmuth
Alfred Rode. Second violinist, Berlin Philharmonic
Orchestra since 1935. What's it mean, second violinist,
Helmuth?

Rode It means I wasn't good enough to be a first violinist.

*He chuckles, looks round for approval; Arnold grins
encouragingly.*

Mind you, you have to be pretty good just to be a second
violinist in the Berlin Philharmonic. Even though I say so
myself.

Arnold And according to your questionnaire, Helmuth,
you never joined the Party.

Rode Me? Never. Never.

Long silence. Arnold just watches him and waits.

I hated them. Believe me, please, I know everyone says
now they were never Nazis, but in my case it is absolutely
one hundred per cent true. I am a Catholic, a convert,
it would have been totally against my conscience.

Silence.

It's difficult to explain what it was like. Terror, that's what you felt from morning till night, even asleep, you felt terror.

Brief silence.

In the early days, of course, we were much more open in opposition. I'm talking about '33, '34. When I think back on the things I said, I shudder. My God, I used to tell jokes, anti-Hitler jokes, I was well known for my anti-Hitler jokes. For example, this joke, it was very famous around '33, '34. A couple of old Jews. One says to the other, 'I have two bits of news for you, one good, one bad.' 'Tell me the good news first.' 'Hitler's dead.' 'And the bad news?' 'It isn't true.'

He chuckles; looks round; nothing from the others.

That's the sort of joke I used to tell.

Silence; he wipes sweat from his brow.

You want to know about Dr Furtwängler? This man is without doubt one of the most courageous people it has been my honour to know. We all acknowledge he is a god among musicians. In my humble, second-violinist opinion, the greatest conductor alive. True, I have not played under Arturo Toscanini, but I have heard his recordings, and the emotion is not the same. Toscanini is a metronome. Dr Furtwängler is an artist. No, no. Wilhelm Furtwängler is unquestionably a genius, without equal.

Silence; he loosens his coat, wipes his brow again.

Is it true you're going to interview him today?

Silence.

Berlin is so full of rumours. I heard –

Silence; smiles.

You hear things all the time. If rumours were edible we'd all be well fed. If I may say so, I hope you see to it that he's properly guarded. There are so many crazy people about.

Silence.

He gave comfort in terrible times, what man can do more?

Silence.

Here's something that may interest you. On a famous occasion, I think it was the second Winter Assistance charity programme, an all-Beethoven concert, this was in '35, it was suddenly announced that Hitler himself was going to attend. Well, you can imagine, the Maestro was outraged. You know how angry he was? He ripped the wooden covering off the radiator in his dressing room, that's how angry he was. Because what could he do? He couldn't tell Hitler not to attend.

Chuckles, looks round, silence.

You see, the problem was the Nazi salute. He absolutely refused to give it. Now this I heard him say with my own ears, I heard him say, 'I don't have to acknowledge him at all,' over and over again, I heard him say that. But how could he avoid giving the Devil's salute with Satan actually present in the audience? You know who came up with a solution?

Modestly taps his chest with his thumb.

I said, 'Maestro, why not enter with your baton in your right hand? Hitler will be sitting in the front row. If you give the salute with the baton in your hand, it'll look like you're going to poke his eyes out.' (*Chuckles.*) He was really grateful to me for that suggestion. He came on to the podium, baton in his right hand which meant he couldn't give the salute. He just bowed quickly, turned immediately to us, and even while the audience was still applauding he gave the signal to begin. (*Smiles fondly at the memory.*) I tell you in confidence, after the concert, I did something disreputable. I stole that baton. As a memento of a great act of courage. I still have it. I should have brought it to show you.

Silence.

Mind you, it was always a joke in the orchestra. The Maestro's baton. He has a very eccentric technique. (*Stands and demonstrates.*) He waves, he sways, he jiggles. God knows when you're meant to come in. His downbeat was always the subject of jokes. Other musicians used to ask us, how do you know when to play the first chord of the 'Eroica'? When his baton reaches the third stud on his shirt, we'd say. Or, how do you know when to start the semiquavers at the beginning of the Ninth? We used to tell them, the moment the Maestro enters, we all walk round our chairs three times, sit down, count to ten and play. Or. When we lose patience.

Chuckles, sits again; silence.

Yet he can produce musical sounds like no other human being alive. (*To Emmi.*) I hope I'm not going too fast for you, Fräulein –?

Emmi Straube.

Rode Straube. Any relation to Colonel Joachim Straube?

Emmi My father.

Rode rises.

Rode I am deeply honoured to be in your presence, Fräulein Straube. Your father was a true patriot. A man of God. *Requiescat in pacem.*

He crosses himself, sits; silence.

No, no, I want to say categorically that Wilhelm Furtwängler did not serve the regime. None of us who were members of his orchestra served the regime. Forgive me if I make a philosophical observation, but Wilhelm Furtwängler is a symbol to the entire world of all that is great in culture and music and the Nazis needed him. They needed him to make themselves respectable.

Silence. David raises a discreet finger.

Arnold You have a question for Helmuth, David?

David Yes. There's a photograph, isn't there, Mr Rode, of Dr Furtwängler shaking hands with Hitler. How do you explain that?

Rode But that's the concert I was talking about, the all-Beethoven programme, when he came on with his baton in his right hand to avoid giving the salute. As I said, Hitler was in the front row and at the end of the concert, he suddenly stood up, went to the platform and offered the Maestro his hand. And the Maestro took it – what else could he do? That's all there was to it. I was there. I witnessed it. It was probably a calculated act, not spontaneous at all, because they wanted the Maestro on their side, of course they did, and so they had photographers there, and what could the Maestro do? He simply had to shake Satan's hand. That's all there is to it.

David is about to ask another question but Arnold signals him to wait.

And he did not conduct *Die Meistersinger* at the Party Congress in Nürnberg in 1935. We played it the evening *before* the Congress. The music was quite separate from the politics. That is the Maestro's creed: politics and art must be kept separate. It's the same with the Devil's birthday. It was the evening before, 19th April, not the 20th. And the Maestro was tricked into it. Usually, when they wanted him to conduct on such occasions, he managed to get his doctors to diagnose spondylitis – inflammation of the vertebrae in the back and neck, common in conductors, and very, very painful. But for Satan's birthday in 1942, Goebbels got to the doctors first and that was that. (*Brief pause.*) And don't forget, please, the Maestro had to flee to Switzerland only last year, just before the war ended, because he learned that the Gestapo were about to arrest him. This is an honest, good man we are talking about. And the greatest conductor alive.

Again David raises a finger. Arnold nods.

David Mr Rode, you only joined the Berlin Philharmonic in 1935. Where were you before that?

Rode I was a member of another orchestra. In Mannheim. But in 1935, several vacancies arose in Berlin. I auditioned –

He loses confidence; becomes agitated.

Yes, yes, but on the other hand Dr Furtwängler, personally, was very good to Jews. He helped a lot of Jews escape, Jews who were no longer allowed to be members of the orchestra, although he fought to retain them for as long as he could. His secretary, Berta Geissmar, was a Jewess. He relied so much on her. In the end, he had to help her to escape, too. She is now, I believe, in England, secretary to Sir Thomas Beecham. He's also a conductor but he is not Dr Furtwängler.

Arnold Helmuth, do you know Hans Hinkel?

Rode (*alarmed*) Do I know Hans Hinkel?

Arnold That's what I asked.

Rode Do I know Hans Hinkel?

Arnold You seem to understand the question, Helmuth, now how about answering it?

Rode But how could I know such a man? Hans Hinkel was in the Ministry of Culture, how could I know such a man?

Silence.

I hear he kept this archive, files, records – (*Fishing.*) Do you know what's in the archive, Major?

Arnold I was just going to ask you that, Helmuth.

Rode Me? How should I know what's in the archive?

Silence.

The only thing I've heard is that there are letters from people swearing loyalty to the regime, that's all I know.

Silence.

My personal, second-violinist opinion, for what it's worth, is that Hinkel was in fact a very low level functionary – his archive won't have anything of interest.

Silence.

Arnold Okay, you can go now, Helmuth.

Rode That's it?

Arnold Get out, Helmuth.

Rode rises, bows to all three and goes to the double doors. As he opens them he stops dead, bows deeply to someone in the waiting room.

Rode (*awed*) Maestro!

Emmi rises involuntarily as Rode exits, beaming, closing the door.

Emmi (*equally awed, going to the door*) He's here, Major –

Arnold Sit down, Emmi.

She sits.

We're going to keep him waiting, too. (*To David.*) So now you know the baton story, David.

David Yes, but Captain Greenwood is right. When it comes to hard evidence –

Arnold (*interrupting*) Get us some coffee, Emmi, will you? And, Emmi, don't offer coffee to the leader of the band. Don't even greet him, okay?

Emmi goes.

Jesus, when are they going to fix the central heating? My scrotum feels like a shrivelled prune. Probably looks like one, too.

Rode hurries across the rubble. Tamara stops him, questions him, then both disappear, quickly in opposite directions, Tamara, like a fury, towards the office. Arnold adds wood to the stove.

Let me tell you something, David, the evidence, hard or soft, doesn't matter, because I have the one question he's going to find it impossible to answer.

A commotion in the waiting room. A woman's voice shouting. Arnold goes towards the door but Emmi comes rushing in, highly agitated.

Emmi There's a woman attacking Dr Furtwängler.

Tamara bursts into the room like an avenging angel. She is prematurely grey, intense, driven.

Tamara This is an outrage – who's in charge? I have to see who's in charge –

Overlapping, confused, and at speed:

Arnold Get out of here, who the hell – ?

Tamara Have you any idea who's sitting out there – ? Wilhelm Furtwängler is sitting out there –

Arnold Emmi, call the guard –

Emmi makes for the door but Tamara grabs Emmi and starts to shake her.

Tamara You're crazy, you're all crazy, you don't know what you're doing –

Arnold David, get hold of her

David tries to grab her but she turns on him and starts pounding him with her fists.

Tamara You can't do this, you can't do this –

Just as suddenly she stops, tries to catch her breath, forlorn, distraite. Emmi tries not to whimper.

I'm sorry. When I saw him, I lost all control. Everything went out of my mind.

Arnold Why don't you sit down for a moment, I'll call a medic –

Tamara No, no. I have to talk to you. Are you in charge?

Arnold Who are you?

Tamara My name is Tamara Sachs.

Arnold (*to Emmi*) Isn't this the one I'm seeing at two?

David Sit down, Miss Sachs.

Tamara Mrs Sachs.

David Emmi, get her a glass of water.

Tamara I have something of importance to tell you about Wilhelm Furtwängler.

Silence.

Arnold Okay, Emmi, get us all some coffee.

David Please sit down, Mrs Sachs.

Tamara sits. Emmi exits quickly.

Tamara I told them about it in Wiesbaden. They said I must tell you. Then I heard you were interviewing him today. I have material evidence to give.

Arnold considers for a moment.

Arnold Okay. But just wait for my secretary to come back so she can take a record.

Silence.

Tamara You see, I am trying to find some proof that my husband, Walter Sachs, existed.

Silence.

Dr Furtwängler may be able to provide that proof. I've been waiting since the early hours. Then, when I actually saw him – (*She is lost for a moment.*) Could he come in, please?

Arnold No, he can't come in.

David Was your husband a friend of his?

Tamara No. My husband, Walter Sachs, was the most promising young pianist of his generation.

David Were they colleagues, perhaps?

Tamara No. That's just the point.

Emmi returns with a tray of coffee and cups, flustered but pleased, a little excited.

Emmi Dr Furtwängler spoke to me. He wants to know how long he is to be kept waiting.

Arnold Emmi, put the coffee down, then go out there and tell him in these words, these exact words, mind, tell him, 'You'll wait until Major Arnold's ready to see you or until hell freezes over, whichever takes longer.' You got that, Emmi? And don't say anything else, okay?

Tamara Can't he come in, please?

Arnold Go on, Emmi. Then come back and take notes. I'll do the coffee.

Emmi goes out.

Tamara, how do you take your coffee?

Tamara Is there cream and sugar?

Arnold There is in the American Zone.

He serves her coffee. Emmi returns, sits at her table.

Okay, Tamara, let's hear what you have to say. You handle this, David. You and Tamara seem to have a certain – rapport. I'll just sit here and listen.

David Whatever you say, Mrs Sachs, will be treated as confidential.

Tamara But I don't want it treated as confidential. I want the world to know.

David When I asked if your husband and Dr Furtwängler were colleagues, you said, 'No, that's just the point.' What did you mean exactly?

Tamara (*distraught*) I can't remember what I wanted to say now. It's gone out of my mind. (*She rummages in her handbag.*) I have a list here, why did I bring this list?

David Perhaps it would help if I asked you questions –

Tamara I think Dr Furtwängler is the only man who can give me proof that my husband existed.

David How could he do that?

Tamara I've not been well. For some years now I've not been well. After they took Walter – we were in Paris at the time – I returned here to be near my mother. My father was with the army of occupation in Denmark. I shall be thirty-three next birthday, look at my hair – (*She holds out a strand of hair.*) I'm trying to return to France but the French authorities are not helpful. I want to die in Paris. It was the only place we were happy.

Arnold (*gently*) Tamara, where are you staying? Because I'll have you taken back there and then I can get a doctor to you, and –

Tamara (*to David, ignoring Arnold*) I was a philosophy student in 1932, at the University here in Berlin. I was eighteen years old. I was taken to a recital in a private house to hear a young pianist. The house belonged to Dr Myra Samuel, who was a famous piano teacher of the time. The young pianist was Walter Sachs, aged seventeen. A year younger than me. I fell in love with him just listening to him play. He was very beautiful. We were married. He was a Jew. I am not. My maiden name was Müller.

Arnold Just tell us how Dr Furtwängler figures in all this.

Tamara It's an outrage what you are doing, you know.

Arnold What are we doing?

Tamara Behaving like them.

David What happened to your husband, Mrs Sachs?

Tamara He died. In Auschwitz. That's in Poland. I don't know the exact date.

David And Dr Furtwängler?

Tamara We were tipped off that my husband was to be arrested within the week. We had no money, no influence. We went rushing round to Myra Samuel. We asked for help. She said she'd see what she could do. That evening she sent a message: be at such-and-such an address at midnight. It was a cellar, once a nightclub but closed down. We were terrified. We knocked. Dr Samuel opened the door and admitted us. There was only one other person there. 'This is Wilhelm Furtwängler,' she said. 'He will listen to you play.' There was an old upright piano, a Bechstein, out of tune. Walter sat down and played no more than three minutes of the 'Waldstein' Sonata. Dr Furtwängler suddenly stood. He said, 'I will try to help,' and left quickly. The very next day we received an official permit to leave. We took the train to Paris and we were happy. Walter began to make a name for himself. Then. June, 1940. They took Walter away. I am not Jewish. My maiden name was Müller –

She suddenly remembers something, becomes agitated.

Yes, yes, I have this list – (*Rummages in her handbag again, produces sheets of paper.*) I remember now, these are some of the other people he helped, Jews and non-Jews he helped. (*Reading.*) Ludwig Misch, Felix Lederer, Josef Krips, Arnold Schönberg, dozens and dozens of people he helped. He helped Walter Sachs, my husband, undoubtedly the finest pianist of his generation. I'll find out more, I'll keep asking, I'll write letters, I'll give evidence, because I know what you want to do, you want to destroy him, isn't that true? You want to burn him at the stake –

David We're just trying to find out the truth –

Tamara How can you find out the truth? There's no such thing. Whose truth? The victors? The vanquished? The victims? The dead? Whose truth? No, no. You have only one duty. To determine who is good and who is evil. That's all there is to it. To destroy one good man now is to make the future impossible. Don't behave like them, please. I know what I'm talking about, the good are few and far between. You must honour the good, especially if they are few. Like Dr Furtwängler. And the children of the good. Like Fräulein Straube.

Arnold Gee, Emmi, you're really famous in this city.

Tamara I want to see him, please. I want to know if he remembers Walter. I want to know if he remembers that night Walter played the opening of the 'Waldstein' Sonata on an out-of-tune Bechstein upright piano in a Berlin cellar.

David looks enquiringly at Arnold.

Arnold Tamara, not today. We have to talk to your benefactor first, you see?

Tamara You're going to set fire to him, aren't you?

Arnold Ah, c'mon, Tamara, I'm only an investigating officer. I don't have the power to set fire to anybody. Even if I wanted to. Which I don't. Believe me. Here's what we'll do. Emmi's going to take you out the back way and she's going to get Sergeant Bonelli to drive you to wherever you want to go. (*Writes on a piece of paper.*) This is my number. I want you to call me if you need anything, I mean

anything, food, cigarettes, medicine, anything, okay?
How's that sound?

Tamara It sounds as if you're going to burn him.

Arnold Emmi, take Tamara out the back way.

*Emmi starts to take Tamara to the door but Tamara
stops.*

Tamara Would you like this list? I have a copy.

Arnold You keep it, Tamara, and the copy. But thanks
a lot.

*She goes quickly, followed by Emmi. Arnold gives a
yelp of triumph.*

Jesus Christ! Are we going to nail him! We're going to
nail him good and proper –

He stops, noticing David's bewildered expression.

You don't see it, do you?

David No, I don't see how a list of people whom he's
supposed to have helped –

Arnold David, last month I was in Vienna. I had with me
an Austrian driver, Max his name was, he'd done time in
the camps. We were looking at these Viennese cleaning
up the bomb damage, scavenging for rotting food, butt
ends, anything. I said, 'To think, a million of these people
came out to welcome Adolf on the day he entered the
city, a million of them, and now look at 'em.' And Max
said, 'Oh, not these people, Major. These people were all
at home hiding Jews in their attics.' You get the point,
David? The point is they're all full of shit.

David If I may say so, Major, I think Dr Furtwängler's
in a different category. He is, after all, one of the most
famous conductors in the world –

ACT ONE

Arnold (*interrupting*) I'm going to tell you another story,
David. Before I got this assignment, I was at Ike's
headquarters, interrogating prisoners of war. Then they
sent for me. They said, 'You ever heard of Wilhelm
Furtwängler?' 'No,' I said. 'You heard of Toscanini?'
'Sure,' I said. 'You heard of Stockowski?' 'Yeah,' I said,
'I heard of him, old guy with white hair, looks like Harpo
Marx's grandpa.' 'That's the one,' they said, 'and this guy
Furtwängler's bigger than both of them.' 'I get it,' I said,
'the guy's a band leader.' They laughed, oh boy, they
really laughed. They said, well, he may be more than
that, Steve. In this neck of the woods he's probably Bob
Hope and Betty Grable rolled into one. 'Jeez,' I said, 'and
I never heard of him.' And you know what they said next?
They said, 'Steve, that's why you get the job.'

David Who's 'they', Major?

Arnold Who's 'they' what?

David Who's the 'they' that sent for you? Who's the
'they' that gave you this assignment?

Arnold There's no 'the they', David. I'm just doing my
job. And always remember we're dealing here with
degenerates, that's all you got to remember. I seen things
with these eyes –

He shudders. David watches him.

David Major –

Arnold Steve, c'mon, please –

David Don't treat me as if I'm not on your side.

Arnold Well, I do that, David, because I don't yet know
what side you're on.

David I think that's insulting –

113

Arnold Tough. Hank Greenwood gave me the same
feeling. He was interested in justice, evidence, facts. I'm
interested in nailing the bastard –

Emmi returns.

Did Bonelli find her transport?

Emmi Yes.

Arnold Okay. This is it. Emmi, go get him.

Emmi exits.

Same rules of engagement. I'll explain why he's here, then
I'll ask two questions. And then we'll wait. (*Sits at his
desk.*) Oh boy, have I been looking forward to this.

Emmi reappears.

Emmi Dr Wilhelm Furtwängler.

*Wilhelm Furtwängler, wearing a well-cut but worn
overcoat, enters. He is sixty, arrogant and remote, but
at the moment irritated at having been kept waiting.
As he passes her, Emmi gives him a small curtsey, no
more than a bob. David inclines his head, a sort of
bow. Furtwängler glances round, sees the visitor's chair
and sits in it. Arnold looks up.*

Arnold Wilhelm, I didn't hear anyone invite you to sit
down.

Furtwängler stands. Arnold points to the other chair.

Sit there.

Furtwängler sits in the witness chair.

I'm Steve Arnold. This is David Wills.

Arnold consults a file.

Now, Wilhelm, I want you to understand why you're here. You're automatically banned from public life under Control Council Directive No. 24. We're looking into your case before you appear in front of the Tribunal of Artists of the Denazification Commission. You understand that?

Furtwängler I have already been cleared by a denazification tribunal in Austria.

Arnold What they do in Austria doesn't interest me one little bit. Okay? I have your questionnaire here. (*Reading.*) 'Gustav Heinrich Ernst Martin Wilhelm Furtwängler, born Berlin, January 1886. Orchestral conductor.' And you say here you never joined the Party.

Furtwängler That is correct.

A very long silence. Arnold waits; nothing from Furtwängler. When the silence is unbearable Arnold explodes.

Arnold Jesus Christ, aren't you going to tell us about carrying your baton in your right hand so you wouldn't have to salute and poke Adolf's eyes out?

Nothing from Furtwängler.

And aren't you going to tell us about being a Prussian Privy Councillor? How did that happen to a non-Party member?

Furtwängler I received a telegram from Hermann Göring who was Prime Minister of Prussia, this was in 1933, informing me that he had made me a Privy Councillor. I was not given the opportunity either to accept or to refuse. After the dreadful events of November '38, the violent attacks against Jews, I stopped using the title.

Arnold Great, great, you stopped using the title, and
what about Vice-President of the Chamber of Music, you
used that title, didn't you, but then I suppose you had no
choice there either, because I suppose Josef just sent you
a telegram saying, 'Dear Mr Vice-President.'

Furtwängler No. I don't think Goebbels sent me a
telegram. I was simply told. In a letter, I think. I don't
remember exactly –

Arnold You don't remember exactly, okay, but, hell,
Hermann and Josef were sure heaping honours on you.
One makes you a Privy Councillor, the other makes you
Vice-President of the Chamber of Music, and you weren't
even a member of the Party, how do you explain that?

Furtwängler There was a constant battle between Göring
and Goebbels as to which of them would control Nazi
culture. People like me, and Richard Strauss, were simply
in the middle. We were pawns. Anyway, I resigned from
the Chamber of Music at the same time as I resigned as
Musical Director of the Berlin Philharmonic Orchestra.
In 1934.

David Why was that? Why did you resign, Dr
Furtwängler?

Arnold shoots David a sharp look of annoyance.

Furtwängler They came to power in January '33. In
April, I wrote an open letter to the newspapers
condemning what they were doing to music, making
these distinctions between Jews and non-Jews. For my
part, the only divide in art is between good and bad.
Great artists are rare, I said, and no country can do
without them unless it wishes to damage its cultural life
irrevocably. I also said that men like Otto Klemperer,
Bruno Walter, Max Reinhardt, I may have mentioned

others, I don't remember now, must be allowed to serve their art here in this country.

David And then you resigned?

Furtwängler No, not then. Those were early days. No, the matter came to a head when Goebbels decided to ban *Mathis the Painter*, an opera by Paul Hindemith. They called it Jew-infected Bolshevik music, or some such nonsense. Again I wrote to the newspapers. Again I criticised them. Goebbels retaliated with a speech in which he denounced me for what he called my 'disloyalty to the regime'. That's when I resigned. I resigned everything. I simply withdrew from public life and started composing again, which I'd always thought was my true vocation. Eventually, after much toing and froing, I was summoned by Goebbels. He said I could leave the country if I wanted to but under no condition would I ever be allowed to return. That would have been a victory for them. I believe you have to fight from inside not from without. He then demanded I acknowledge Hitler as solely responsible for cultural policy. Well, that was a fact. He was the sole arbiter and it seemed to me pointless to deny it. In return, I demanded I be allowed to stay here, to work, but I would not be obliged to accept any official position. Nor would I have to perform at state functions. I have always held the view that art and politics should have nothing to do with each other.

Arnold Oh, really? Then why did you conduct at one of their Nürnberg rallies?

Furtwängler (*flaring*) I did not conduct at the rally, I conducted on the evening *before* the rally –

Arnold That sounds like the small print in one of our insurance policies, Wilhelm –

Furtwängler I had nothing to do with the rally.

Arnold And what about April 19th, 1942? The eve of Adolf's fifty-third birthday, the big night, the big celebration – you conducted for Adolf, didn't you? Was that in keeping with your view that art and politics have nothing to do with each other?

Furtwängler (*flustered*) That was a different matter –

Arnold I'll believe that –

Furtwängler I was tricked –

Arnold How come?

Furtwängler I was in Vienna, rehearsing the Ninth Symphony of Beethoven with the Vienna Philharmonic when Goebbels called and said I had to conduct at Hitler's birthday. Always, I'd managed to wriggle out of such invitations, pleading previous engagements, illness, and so on. I was also fortunate that Baldur von Schirach, who controlled Vienna, hated Goebbels and would do anything to thwart his wishes. He had often helped me in the past by saying, for example, that he had the prior claim on my services. But on this particular occasion, in 1942, Goebbels got to my doctors before me, they were frightened off, and von Schirach was threatened and bullied and gave in. I had no alternative but to conduct for Hitler. Believe me, I knew I had compromised, and I deeply regret it.

Arnold (*playing with him*) Von Schirach, von Schirach. Is that the same Baldur von Schirach, the Nazi Youth Leader, who's now sitting in the dock at Nürnberg, on trial for his life, charged with crimes against humanity?

No response.

So that's how you were 'tricked', huh? Doesn't sound much of a trick to me.

Furtwängler To the best of my knowledge that is what happened. The trick was that pressure was brought to bear before I was able to manoeuvre. The regime knew as well as I did that I had not bowed my knee.

Arnold It doesn't sound like that to me. It sounds like you made a deal –

Furtwängler I made no deal. My only concern was preserving the highest musical standards. That I believe to be my mission.

Arnold I don't buy that –

Furtwängler It's the truth –

Arnold Do you remember a pianist called Walter Sachs?

Furtwängler No.

Arnold A young, Jewish pianist?

Furtwängler No.

Arnold A pupil of – (*To Emmi.*) What was the teacher's name?

Emmi Myra Samuel –

Furtwängler I knew Myra Samuel –

Arnold And you don't remember this pupil of hers playing to you in a cellar, here in Berlin?

Furtwängler Vaguely. What was his name?

Arnold Walter Sachs.

Furtwängler Sachs, Sachs –

Arnold His widow attacked you a minute ago –

Furtwängler No one's attacked me –

Arnold In the waiting room –

Furtwängler But that woman didn't attack me. She was trying to kiss my hand.

Arnold Right. Right. I guess that was because she's grateful to you. She wanted to thank you for helping her husband. You got him a permit to leave for Paris. How did you do that, Wilhelm?

Furtwängler I can't remember. There were so many.

Arnold Yeah, yeah, we've heard about all the folks you helped. I'm just interested in how you went about it. Did you call someone you knew?

Furtwängler I may have, as I say, I simply don't remember.

Arnold Let me guess then. You picked up the phone and made a call. (*Mimes a telephone.*) 'Hi, Adolf? Wilhelm speaking. Listen, old pal, there's a Jew-boy pianist I want you to help. He needs a permit to get to Paris. Gee, that's swell of you, Adolf. Shall I have him pick it up or will you send it round? God bless you, Adolf, and Heil fucking Hitler!'

Emmi sticks her fingers in her ears and shuts her eyes tight.

Or maybe you called Hermann or Josef? Because, you see, I think you made a deal, you shook hands with the Devil and you became real close to him and his cohorts. You were so close you were in the same shithouse as them, you could wipe their asses for them –

He suddenly notices Emmi.

Emmi, how the hell can you take notes with your goddam fingers –? Emmi!

She removes her fingers.

This is Emmi Straube, Wilhelm. She's a very sensitive girl.

Furtwängler gives her a nod.

So, Wilhelm, how many Jews do you think you helped?

Furtwängler I have no idea.

Arnold That many, huh?

Furtwängler I am not going to defend myself by trumpeting numbers. May I ask a question?

Arnold Sure.

Furtwängler When will my case be heard by the Tribunal?

Arnold Your guess is as good as mine.

Furtwängler I recently visited your colleagues in Wiesbaden, the American Occupation Authorities, those charged with assisting my defence, they were extremely polite and helpful. They said they –

Arnold This isn't Wiesbaden. And I'm not here to defend you –

Furtwängler I need to work. I need to make my living. I have been living off the generosity of friends –

Arnold Tough, but these things take time –

Furtwängler (*growing more and more agitated*) Then why is it, please, that – that – another conductor who was actually a member of the Party, I believe he joined twice, why has he already been cleared and is working again, while I have to wait and wait and wait?

Arnold I don't know who he is, he wasn't my case –

Furtwängler And why is it, please, that on good authority I have learned that certain high-ranking Nazi scientists are, even as we speak, being transported to the United States to work on missiles and rocket fuels?

Arnold That's what we call the spoils of war, Wilhelm. Different professions, different rules. Why did you escape to Switzerland in January last year?

Furtwängler What?

Arnold Why did you escape to Switzerland last year?

Furtwängler Because I learned that the Gestapo were about to arrest me.

Arnold Why were they going to arrest you?

Furtwängler I'm not absolutely sure but I believe it was because of another letter I'd written to Goebbels lamenting the decline of musical standards due to racial policies.

Arnold You didn't complain about the racial policies, just about the decline of musical standards, is that right?

No response.

So, how did you learn that the Gestapo was out to get you?

Furtwängler During an enforced hour-long interval, because of a power failure at a concert in the Blüthner Hall, here, in Berlin, Albert Speer, the Minister of Armaments, said to me, casually, 'You look very tired, Maestro, you should go abroad for a while.' I understood exactly what he meant.

Arnold (*affecting innocence*) Is that the same Albert Speer who's now sitting beside your other friend, Baldur, in the dock at Nürnberg, also charged with crimes against humanity?

No response.

You sure knew a lot of people in high places.

Furtwängler It would be truer to say that a lot of people in high places knew me.

Arnold Don't get smart with me, because your friends seem to be just a bunch of criminal shitheads. But I know and you know that you were real close to all of them, to Adolf and Hermann and Josef and Baldur and now Albert. Make a call, a Jew is saved. Write a nasty letter, Albert says leave town. So, let's hear the truth, Wilhelm, let's come clean. What was your Party number?

Furtwängler If you are going to bully me like this, Major, then you had better do your homework. You obviously have no idea how stupid and impertinent your remarks are.

Arnold (*stung*) You remember, David, I said I had a question for Wilhelm that he wouldn't be able to answer. Well, I'm going to ask it now. You ready for this, Wilhelm? Take your time, it's a tough one. Why didn't you get out right at the start when Adolf came to power in 1933? I have some names here, people in your line of business, who got out in '33. Bruno Walter, Otto Klemperer –

Furtwängler But they were Jews, they had to leave, they were right to leave.

Brief silence.

I love my country and my people. That is a matter of body and soul. I could not leave my country in her deepest misery. To have left in 1933 or '34 would have been shameful. I remained here to give comfort, to see that the glorious musical tradition, of which I believe I am one of the guardians, remained unbroken, was intact when we woke from the nightmare. I remained because I believed my place was with my people.

Arnold See, David? He can't answer the question. I'll ask it again, Wilhelm, and don't give me any more airy-fairy bullshit –

Furtwängler (*flaring, at his most arrogant*) I have told you my reasons, and I only hope, Major, you will be as hard on other artists who have remained in their countries. Shostakovich, Prokofiev, Eisenstein, especially Eisenstein with his films glorifying tyranny, but you could accuse them all of glorifying tyranny –

Arnold I never heard of them, they're not on my list –

David No, they're Russians –

Arnold Russians? (*Laughs.*) Yeah, Russians –

The telephone rings.

Emmi (*into telephone*) Major Arnold's office. (*Listens.*) It's Major Richards for Lieutenant Wills.

David (*taking the telephone*) Wills. (*Listens.*) Yes. You want me to tell him? Yup. (*To Arnold.*) Major Richards wants a word.

Arnold goes to the small table with the telephone extension. Emmi waits for him to pick up, then puts down her receiver. Furtwängler rises.

Furtwängler I have had enough of this. I am leaving now.

David I don't think that would be advisable.

Furtwängler hesitates and doesn't leave. Arnold yelps with delight and then laughs. David summons his courage.

Dr Furtwängler.

Furtwängler turns to him. David feels awkward but takes the plunge as though he's been preparing a speech.

When I was ten, in 1932, my father, he was a publisher, allowed me to accompany him on a business trip to Berlin. On the second evening of our visit, he took me to the Philharmonic. I can't remember the whole programme but I do remember you conducted both Beethoven's *Egmont* overture and the Fifth Symphony. I think the concert ended with the overture to *Tannhaüser*. You opened a new world to me –

Another yelp and laughter from Arnold. David falters, searching now for the words.

More than a world. Like waking from sleep. A child of ten. Waking to a new world. You showed me a place where there was – an absence of misery. Ever since I first heard you, music has been central to my life. My chief comfort. And I've needed comfort. I thank you for that.

He stops, embarrassed, turns away. Furtwängler nods, smiles sadly. Again Arnold laughs.

Emmi I, too. The same. Thank you.

Furtwängler gives her a wonderful smile. She looks away.

Furtwängler Fräulein –?

Emmi Straube.

Furtwängler *Wann haben* Sie *mich zum ersten mal als Dirigent erlebt?*

Emmi (*mumbling*) *Hier. In Berlin. Neunzehnhundert-dreiundvierzig* –

Furtwängler (*not having heard, gently*) *Wann?*

Arnold puts down the telephone, dangerously pleased with himself.

Arnold I've got to hand it to the British, David. You know what those guys are? Decent. Wilhelm, tell me, do you know Hans Hinkel?

Furtwängler Do I know Hans Hinkel?

Arnold Why does everybody repeat my questions?

Furtwängler Do I know Hans Hinkel?

Arnold See? There he goes again –

Furtwängler Yes, I know him. A despicable human being. Ask Bruno Walter. It was Hinkel who personally drove him out. You know what his job was in the Ministry of Culture? To get rid of Jews in the arts, and since the most talented artists were inevitably Jewish, he was seldom idle. I could detail his persecution of my former secretary, Berta Geissmar, herself a Jewess, but I will not bore you with a chronicle of cruelty, meanness and mendacity.

Arnold Yup, sounds like the same guy. You know what else this little creep did? He kept files, close on 250,000 files. And you know what's in those files?

Furtwängler How should I know –?

Arnold Oh boy, you're going to love this. Those files contain – wait for this – the details of every artist working in this country for – guess who? That's right, Wilhelm, your old pals, Adolf and Josef and Hermann. These files are going to tell us when all of you joined the Party, who informed and who was helpful and, what's more, they're full of love letters to your aforementioned pals, swearing everlasting loyalty. Isn't that something? A file on every one of you. Some guy, that Hinkel.

Furtwängler I should like to leave now.

Arnold I bet you would, so why don't you? See, we have work to do sifting through those files, and that'll take some time, I guess. So, get out of here. And we'll call you back when we're good and ready.

Furtwängler goes to the door but stops, turns to Emmi and gives a bow and a smile, then goes. Arnold hurries to his desk.

We've got him! See how the moment I mentioned Hinkel he wanted out? Boy, oh boy! Emmi, give David a list of the witnesses, and get us some more coffee, will you? David, here's what I want you to do.

He finds files and hands them to David.

These are pretty well verbatims of my interrogations. We'll compare the answers the shitheads gave me with the info in Hinkel's files. This is an Aladdin's cave. Jesus, when you think the Russians had the whole archive in their hands until the city was divided and they didn't know what it was. You know what they'll be doing now? Shitting razor blades.

During this, Emmi, on her way to the door, has put on a record and then turns up the volume: the opening of Beethoven's Eighth Symphony at full blast. She goes quickly.

Arnold Hey, turn that off, we can't hear ourselves think. (*Looks up, realises she's gone.*) David, turn that off.

David pretends not to hear.

Shit.

Arnold rises, crosses to the record player and as he takes off the record the music stops abruptly.

Blackout.

Act Two

SCENE ONE

April. Ten p.m. Warm spring evening. Dim light from the desk lamp.

Rode stands in the double doorway, having just greeted Arnold. He wears a tattered cardigan over a short-sleeved shirt and slacks.

Arnold is at his desk which is covered in paper. He is inwardly excited, his mood dangerous. Rode carries a slender leather case.

Rode (*beaming*) Major, you must now guess what I am holding in my hand.

Arnold Your dick.

Rode No, no, come now, guess. You like guessing games?

Arnold Love 'em. I give up, what you holding in your hand, Helmuth?

Rode (*glancing round nervously*) No Fräulein Straube?

Arnold No. That's because I wanted to see you alone, Helmuth. Off the record. So what you got there?

Rode You can't guess?

He opens the leather case.

Arnold Helmuth, I think I know what it is.

Rode What?

Arnold A telescope. For spying on people. Right?

Rode (*a little uneasy, a nervous smile*) No, no, no, not at all.

He takes from the case a conductor's baton.

Arnold (*toying with him*) By Jimminy! A white stick. For the blind!

Rode No, Major, not a white stick, a baton. A conductor's baton. And not just *a* baton. *The* baton. My guilty secret. The Maestro's baton which I stole.

Arnold The one he kept in his right hand.

Rode You remember!

Arnold How could I forget? (*Taking the baton.*) Will you look at this? I'm holding the baton he kept in his right hand so he didn't have to salute and poke Adolf's eyes out. (*Suddenly thrusting it at Rode.*) Show me, Helmuth.

Rode Show you?

Arnold Yeah, show me. I want to see you do it. C'mon, Helmuth, take the baton.

Rode reluctantly takes the baton. Arnold gets out a comb, flicks a lock of hair over his forehead and holds the comb under his nose to make a Hitler moustache.

Pretend I'm Adolf. You're the Maestro. C'mon. You've got the baton in your right hand but you give me the salute just the same.

Rode No, really, Major, I don't like giving the salute even in –

Arnold (*sweetly*) Do it, Helmuth.

Rode gives a half-hearted salute.

Do it right, Helmuth.

Rode gives the salute.

You look great doing that, Helmuth, and I see what you mean. You almost poked my eyes out.

Rode Exactly.

He puts the baton back in the case and gives it to Arnold.

Perhaps you will do me a favour, Major. If you are seeing the Maestro again, be so good as to return the baton to him. It is, after all, his property. But please don't tell him who took it.

Arnold Don't worry, Helmuth, it'll be our secret.

Rode In the meantime, you can practise conducting. I saw you had some of our records. (*He glances at the records.*) I am on this one, the Ninth, second fiddle, difficult to identify me exactly. (*He chuckles.*) You're working late tonight. You don't usually see people this late –

Arnold All in the cause of humanity, Helmuth. Or should I call you one-zero-four-nine-three-three-one.

Rode (*shaken*) What?

Arnold One-zero-four-nine-three-three-one. Or d'you mind if I just call you 'one'?

An agonising silence: then Rode breaks down and sobs.

You know what I say you are, Helmuth? I say you're a piece of shit.

Rode (*through his sobs*) The bastard, the bastard –

Arnold Who's the bastard, Helmuth? Hinkel?

Rode nods.

Why? Well, why particularly?

Rode He said – he said there'd be no records – no file –

Arnold He promised to remove your file?

No response.

And you thought we'd never find out.

No response.

You thought we'd never find out that you were the Party's man in the orchestra? Hinkel's man.

Rode sobs.

Oh, don't take on so, Helmuth. You've only got one Party number. A guy called Herbert von Karajan's got two. (*He laughs.*) By the way, why d'you think he joined the Party twice? Once in Austria, once here? Guess he just wanted them to know he cared, huh?

No response.

So, c'mon, Party member one-zero-four-nine-three-three-one, talk to me.

Rode (*trying to regain his dignity*) I – I – have confessed my sins. I have been given absolution.

Arnold Yeah, but don't you guys have to do penance? What's your penance, Helmuth?

Rode Living out the rest of my life.

Arnold Hold it, your story moves me deeply, let me wipe away my tears. I'm so choked up, I can't speak.

Rode (*burst of anger*) You don't know what it's like to wake up to a power so terrifying, so immense, that all you can think of is you have to be part of it, otherwise you will be eaten alive. And here's something else you won't understand. Absolute power offers absolute certainty and absolute hope.

Arnold Doesn't matter if I understand or not, just get it off your chest, Helmuth.

Rode And you will never have even the slightest inkling of how corrupt the power was; yes, corrupt and corrupting. You have never experienced a Reign of Terror, so there is no way I can make it clear to you. You start by censoring what you say, then you censor what you think, and you end by censoring what you feel. That is the greatest degradation because it means the entire individual will is paralysed, and all that remains is an obedient husk. In my case – (*He breaks off.*)

Arnold Yeah, go on, Helmuth, in your case –?

Rode It began with a realisation.

Arnold And what was that, Helmuth?

Rode That I am not the best violinist in the world.

Arnold You're not?

Rode I would never, in my wildest dreams, have been even a second violinist in the Berlin Philharmonic. When they got rid of the – the Jews in the orchestra there were vacancies for people like me. I believed that to be just. I can trace my ancestry back to the thirteenth century.

Arnold I'm told a lot of Jews can go back even further than that.

Rode (*suddenly agitated*) I lied about something.

Arnold You surprise me, Helmuth.

Rode No, no, I have to set the record straight. I told you it was my idea the Maestro should carry the baton in his right hand. Well, it wasn't my idea at all. The idea came from Franz Jastrau. He was the orchestra's handyman.

Arnold Gee, that sure changes the whole picture, Helmuth.

Rode I don't think the Maestro even knows of my existence. Second violin. A conductor is also a dictator, you know, he is also a terrifying power who gives hope and certainty, and guarantees order. I wanted to be in the Maestro's power, too. The orchestra is a symbol, you see –

Arnold No more philosophy, please, Helmuth, because I want to talk to you about something practical. You ever heard of plea bargaining?

Rode shakes his head.

Talk about power, I have the power to let you go find work, at least in the American Zone. I could give you a job tomorrow, here, in this building. But I'd have to get something in return. See, Helmuth? That's plea bargaining.

Silence.

I have to admit, I thought I'd find a great big fat file on the Maestro. I thought, never mind two Party numbers, he'd have three. But his file is just full of letters asking Josef to help this Jew or that Jew.

Rode Yes, they used to say, there was not a Jew left in Germany whom Furtwängler had not helped.

Arnold C'mon, Helmuth, I can hand you a letter giving you freedom of movement, freedom to work – freedom, Helmuth. Better than scavenging for food in the ruins. But I need something in return. How's that for penance?

Rode He is an anti-Semite. Of course.

Arnold (*gently; wheedling*) Of course. But I need facts, Helmuth, hard facts. You have to tell me where to look.

Rode Major, we're discussing a man of genius here, I don't want – He's one of the greatest conductors alive, maybe *the* greatest –

Arnold Fuck that, Helmuth. You want to discuss symbols here? This guy was a front man. He was the piper but he played their tune, you get my philosophical meaning? I'm not interested in small fish, I'm after Moby Dick. Come on, Helmuth. At least tell me what to look for and where to look for it. Hard facts.

Rode You ever heard of Vittorio de Sabata?

Arnold No.

Rode Italian.

Arnold You're kidding.

Rode A conductor. Front rank. Furtwängler said something like, 'It's impudent for that Jew Sabata to conduct Brahms.'

Arnold Doesn't knock me out that, Helmuth.

Rode There's a letter –

Arnold Now I'm hearing music, I like letters.

Rode It must be in the files somewhere – to Cultural Minister Bernhard Rust, I think – full of – full of the sort of thing you're looking for – about Arnold Schönberg – a Jew – you know who I mean?

Arnold shakes his head.

A composer – modern – atonal.

Arnold What's the date of the letter?

Rode I'll have to think, early I guess, before the war, but – but there's something else I just remembered –

Arnold Yeah?

Rode Furtwängler sent Hitler a birthday telegram –

Arnold He did?

Rode Yes. Oddly enough, I had this from one of your people –

Arnold From one of my people?

Rode Yes. A Corporal. US Army. A Jew. He said he'd seen the telegram. In the Chancellery.

Arnold Son of a gun. We'll find the corporal and we'll find the telegram –

Rode I don't remember his name, but I'll think, it'll come back to me –

Arnold I want you to write all this down, Helmuth.

Puts a pad and pen before him.

And I want you to think about this. I just know a deal was made, early on. They said, 'Wilhelm, you don't have to join the Party, but just do as we tell you and you won't have to worry about a goddam thing.' And that's why he never left. But I need documentary proof. You know of anything like that?

Rode No. And if I may say so, Major, I think you're barking up the wrong tree.

Arnold Oh? And what's the right tree, Helmuth?

Rode There's a pattern to his behaviour, you see. Goebbels understood. And Hinkel. I can tell you things – there's a rumour – I don't know if it's true or not – but ask him about von der Nüll.

Arnold Never heard of him, who is he?

Rode Edwin von der Null. A music critic. He was the
one who gave Furtwängler terrible reviews while he raved
about Herbert von Karajan, the two-time member of the
Party. Called him 'The Miracle Karajan'. Furtwängler
was outraged and they say he had von der Null conscripted
into the army. The same thing happened to another critic,
Walter Steinhauer. He savaged Furtwängler in print for
not playing more contemporary music. After that review
appeared, he too was conscripted. True or not, it's not
such a bad idea. Critics give you bad reviews, you have
them sent to the Russian front. (*Chuckles.*) But if you
really want to get Furtwängler, ask him about Herbert
von Karajan.

Arnold This Miracle Kid?

Rode Yes, that, I believe, will prove fruitful.

He starts to write.

Yes, ask him about von Karajan. And you may notice
that he cannot even bring himself to utter the name.
Furtwängler refers to him as K. And ask him about his
private life.

Arnold His private life?

Blackout.

SCENE TWO

*Mid-July, 8.45 a.m. High summer. Intense heat. Arnold is
at his desk. He is half-asleep, head lolling. He suddenly
wakes and cries out. He becomes aware of his
surroundings, stares into space with a distant, forlorn
expression. Emmi enters carrying a record album. She is
glowing.*

Emmi I've got it, Major.

Arnold Swell.

Emmi The British were most helpful. They really have a broadcasting station there. And they found it for me. Took no more than ten minutes. Amazing. And I am so pleased you are becoming interested in serious music, Major.

Arnold Don't let one record fool you, Emmi.

Emmi But Bruckner's Seventh Symphony, that's difficult even for me. Should we play it now?

Arnold No, Emmi, not now. You know what they mean by the 'slow movement'?

Emmi Of course.

Arnold That's the one I want to hear. Put it on ready to play, and I'll tell you when to play it.

Emmi I never thought you would ask to listen to Bruckner –

Arnold Well, maybe I'm mellowing. Or maybe the heat's getting to me. And, wouldn't you know it? We shiver through a God-awful winter and now the sun's shining the central heating's working. The military, God bless 'em. No sign of the band leader?

Emmi I wish you'd call him Dr Furtwängler. No, he isn't here, but then it's not yet nine o'clock. (*She peers at him.*) Are you nervous, Major?

Arnold I wish you'd call me Steve, Emmi. No, I'm not nervous, I'm just not getting enough sleep. Bad dreams. And that's when I'm awake.

He smiles; she sits at her desk.

137

Now, Emmi, if you want to be out of the room while
I talk to him that's okay by me. What I have to say to
him may upset you. And, I guess, working for me, you
get upset enough.

Emmi What are you going to say to him, Major?

Arnold Emmi, go for a walk. It's a lovely day out there.
Walk in the Tiergarten, sit under what's left of the linden
trees. David can take notes.

Emmi Major, you upset me when you avoid answering
my questions.

A knock at the door.

Arnold See who it is, Emmi, and if it's the band leader
don't let him in yet.

*Emmi opens the door to Rode, who is dressed in a
janitor's overall and cap that somehow looks like a
uniform. He carries a small but bulging canvas sack.
He bows.*

Attention! Security! Watch out, Emmi, he may want to
frisk you.

Rode Major, a woman left this for you.

Arnold What woman?

Rode I don't know her name. She talked to Sergeant
Adams on the door and he gave me this and said it was
for you.

Arnold Did you see her?

Rode Of course. I was standing here, Sergeant Adams
was there, the woman was no more than –

Arnold (*interrupting*) What she look like?

138

Rode shrugs.

Old, young, fat, thin, short, tall?

Rode No.

Rode chuckles.

Arnold Okay, very funny, so what's in the package?

Rode I don't know, Major. Sergeant Adams said it was for you –

Arnold Jesus Christ, Helmuth, you're supposed to be the security in this building –

Rode But I was not told to open packages addressed to military personnel –

Arnold Security, Helmuth, use your goddam common sense –

Rode Sergeant Adams said I must search people, he did not say I must search packages –

Arnold Jesus Christ, no wonder you were a second violinist. I mean, it stands to reason. A woman leaves a package for me, you got to be curious as to what's in it –

Rode Why should I be curious? It's addressed to you, Major –

Arnold Because it could be a fucking bomb, Helmuth.

Rode A bomb? You think so?

Arnold Yes, I think so. Open it.

Rode hesitates.

That's an order, Helmuth. Open it.

Rode hesitates. Emmi is apprehensive and ducks a little behind her typewriter. Arnold does not move.

Rode If it's a bomb, Major, shouldn't you take cover?

Arnold Open it.

Gingerly, Rode opens the sack.

Well, feel around inside. Go on, Helmuth, feel around.

Rode feels inside the sack.

Rode It just feels like paper, Major.

Arnold Empty it.

Rode is about to do so on Arnold's desk.

On the floor, Helmuth.

Rode empties the sack. Fifty or so envelopes, various sizes and colours, cascade onto the floor.

What the hell's that?

All three look at the envelopes, puzzled.

Rode Could be fan mail, Major. I remember with the Maestro –

Arnold Helmuth, who's going to send *me* fan mail for Chrissake? Jesus! Emmi, take a look. Helmuth, get back on duty. The Russians may launch an attack any moment.

Rode bows smartly and goes. Emmi goes down on her knees and starts to examine the envelopes.

Arnold Well, Emmi?

Emmi They're all addressed to Mrs Tamara Sachs. And they're all open –

Arnold What? I don't get it –

Emmi starts to look at the envelopes, then stops.

Emmi Major, can I ask you something?

Arnold The answer's yes, Emmi, I love you, I want you to marry me, and I want you to be the mother of my children, not necessarily in that order.

Emmi Major!

Arnold What's in those letters, Emmi?

Emmi No, I want to ask you this. Why have you been so kind to Mr Rode and not so kind to Dr Furtwängler?

Arnold Let's just say I'm a democrat. With a small 'd'. I have more sympathy for the little people. What's in those letters, Emmi?

David enters carrying files.

David Good morning.

Arnold Okay, we surrender, the boy scout's here.

David What's going on?

Arnold Seems like Tamara Sachs's sent me her mail.

David Why should she do that?

Arnold I don't know exactly. Emmi's trying to come up with an answer.

David hands Arnold the files.

David These are the last of them, Major.

Arnold Anything good?

David Nothing we didn't know before, but the boys at Wiesbaden have asked me to put some questions to you. And I've found something you're not going to like. I happen to be going through a transcript from the Nürnberg trial –

Emmi Major?

Arnold and David turn to her.

There's one here, unopened. It's addressed, 'To Whom It May Concern'.

Arnold Okay, well, it may concern us, Emmi. Open it. Read it.

While Emmi opens the letter:

(*To David.*) I said the woman was crazy, didn't I say it? Look at that. Only a crazy woman would send her own mail to whom it may concern.

Emmi (*reading*) 'To the American authorities in Wiesbaden and Berlin. The good and the not so good. I have been busy. Here are more than fifty letters confirming what I have already said. Letters, evidence in black and white, from survivors, widows, lovers, friends, people now mostly in America and England, all testifying that Wilhelm Furtwängler was their saviour. Because no one knows when Dr Furtwängler's case will come before the tribunal and because I have unexpectedly received permission from the French authorities to reside in Paris –'

David shoots Arnold a look; Arnold looks blithely innocent.

'– I probably will not be here to give evidence on his behalf, so I have taken copies of these letters. If you destroy them they will still exist.'

Brief silence. Emmi continues to sort through the letters.

Arnold Son of a gun. Thanks, Tamara, it's a shame they're all totally irrelevant.

Emmi There's one here from Dr Furtwängler. (*Reads, translating from the German.*) 'Dear Mrs Sachs, Thank

142

you for your letter. Yes, I remember your husband well. As a matter of fact, I was reminded of him only the other day. I remembered the Bechstein was out of tune. He was indeed a fine pianist. I was deeply distressed to hear of his tragic fate.'

Brief silence.

Arnold Get them up off the floor, Emmi. (*To David.*) You were saying the good guys at Wiesbaden had questions for me?

David (*consulting notes; summoning courage*) They – they don't think there's a case against Dr Furtwängler and they want to know why you're pursuing it.

Arnold Tell them they'll know after they've heard the evidence.

Hands David a fat file.

Take a look through that, you'll see what I mean. Next question.

David (*still tentative*) They think you're being ordered to pursue Dr Furtwängler, and they want to know who's giving the orders and why.

Arnold Oh, I get it, you've been talking to them, haven't you, David? You told them about the 'they' who saw me at Ike's headquarters. I remember you were so interested in who the 'they' were –

David Yes, I was asked, I –

Arnold Well, you tell the good guys in Wiesbaden to mind their own goddam business.

David Are you being ordered, Major?

Arnold What's this about a transcript from Nürnberg?

David Why, Major? Why Dr Furtwängler? Why him?

Arnold Tell me about Nürnberg.

Brief pause. David consults one of his own files.

David Yes. A man called Dahlerus, Birger Dahlerus –

Arnold Burger, his name's Burger? What is he, some kind of short-order cook?

David A Swede, a businessman, he was called to give evidence in Göring's defence –

The door suddenly bursts open and Furtwängler enters.

Furtwängler It is now nine o'clock precisely. I have prepared a statement. I do not intend to be kept waiting again.

Uneasy, tense silence.

Arnold (*dangerously calm*) Wilhelm, don't talk to me as if I was a second violinist. Go back into the waiting room, sit down, and *wait*. Miss Straube will come and get you when I am ready to see you. If you're not there when she comes to get you, I'll have you pulled in by the Military Police. Okay, Wilhelm?

Furtwängler hesitates, loses confidence, turns and marches off. Rode shrugs apologetically and also goes.

(*Incensed, almost losing control.*) Jesus God, that prick, that arrogant prick, who the fuck does he think he is? Who the fuck? Who the fuck?

He paces. Emmi watches him, alarmed.

David Major.

Arnold doesn't seem to hear.

Major.

Arnold stops pacing; David again summons courage.

I have a favour to ask you.

Arnold (*suddenly calm*) Okay, I owe you one.

David When you question him, could I ask you to treat him with more respect?

Arnold With more what? More what?

David Respect –

Arnold That's what I thought you said. Respect? Are you kidding?

David He may just be the greatest conductor of this century and that merits respect.

Arnold Yeah, yeah, great conductor, great artist, that's what everybody keeps telling me, and you know what I say to that?

David I can guess what you say to that, Major –

Arnold You know what I say he is?

David Yes, I think I can guess that, too.

Arnold David, I just don't understand a thing about you. You're a Jew. Are you a Jew?

David Yes, I'm a Jew, I'm also a human being –

Arnold A human being, oh, good, I'm relieved, I thought you were going to say you were a music lover. This man, this great artist has made anti-Semitic remarks like you wouldn't believe, I got letters –

David (*interrupting*) Major, Major.

Arnold is still.

Show me a non-Jew who hasn't made anti-Semitic remarks and I'll show you the gates of paradise.

Arnold What is it with you? Where are your feelings, David? Where's your hatred, your disgust? Where's your fucking outrage, David? Think of your parents and then think of him conducting 'Happy Birthday, Dear Adolf'. I mean, for Chrissake, whose side are you on?

Brief pause.

So what's this about the Swede in Nürnberg?

David It doesn't matter now. It's probably irrelevant.

Brief pause.

Arnold Okay, Emmi. Go get him. Oh, and Emmi. Don't announce him. Just let him come in.

She goes. Uneasy silence while they wait. Emmi opens the door for Furtwängler who re-enters.

Wilhelm! Nice to see you. How are you? Been keeping well? Not too hot for you? Come in, come in, sit down.

Furtwängler, deeply suspicious, goes for the witness chair.

No, no, take this one, it's more comfortable –

Arnold places the visitor's chair and holds it for Furtwängler, who sits.

Isn't this heat something else? You want to loosen your tie, take off your jacket? Just relax, because the good news is that this is the last time you'll have to see me.

Furtwängler eyes him suspiciously.

But the bad news is that I still have to test the case against you, see if it'll stand up, and if it does, then I hand over to the civil authorities, to your own people, a guy called Alex Vogel, you ever heard of him?

Furtwängler Yes, I've heard of him.

Arnold And what have you heard?

Furtwängler That he's a Moscow hack, a communist.

Arnold That's the one. Not a nice man. We are not on first-name terms. So, today, thank your lucky stars, you've only got me to deal with. Now, let's take it nice and easy. Okay? I don't want to go over all the old stuff because I have one or two new things that have come up –

Furtwängler (*interrupting*) I wish to say something.

Arnold Go ahead, be my guest.

Furtwängler (*taking out a piece of paper*) When I last saw you, I was unprepared, I did not know what to expect. In the past weeks, I have been thinking more carefully and making some notes. (*Glances at notes; more to David.*) You have to understand who I am and what I am. I am a musician and I believe in music. I am an artist and I believe in art. You could say that art is my religion. Art in general, and music, of course, in particular, has for me mystical powers which nurture man's spiritual needs. I must confess, however, to having been extremely naive. I insisted for many years, until quite recently in fact, on the absolute separation of art and politics. I truly had no interest in politics, I hardly read newspapers, my entire life was devoted to music because, and this is very important, I believed that I could, through music, preserve something practical.

Arnold And what was that?

Furtwängler Liberty, humanity and justice.

Arnold Gee, Wilhelm, that's a thing of beauty, honest to God, a thing of beauty. I'm going to try to remember that. How's it go? Liberty, humanity and justice. Beautiful. But you used the word 'naive'. Are you now saying you think you were wrong? That art and politics can't be separated?

Furtwängler I believe they should be kept separate, but that they weren't kept separate I learned to my cost.

Arnold And when did you first learn that? When you sent the telegram? Was that the surrender signal, the waving of the white flag?

Furtwängler What telegram?

Arnold 'Happy birthday, dear Adolf, love Wilhelm.' Or words to that effect. That sounds to me like you were dropping on your knees and saying, 'Okay, Adolf, you win. You're top dog in everything, so let's be pals. Have a swell party.' Is that when you decided you couldn't keep art and politics separate, when you sent the telegram?

Furtwängler I have no idea what you're talking about.

Arnold I'm talking about the birthday greetings to your old pal, Adolf.

Furtwängler I never sent him birthday greetings or any other kind of greetings.

Arnold Think carefully, Wilhelm –

Furtwängler I don't have to think carefully. This is utterly ridiculous. I never sent him a telegram.

David, who has been consulting the file Arnold gave him, raises a discreet finger.

Arnold Yes, David?

David (*apparently innocently*) Why not show Dr Furtwängler the evidence? It may refresh his memory.

Arnold shoots David a sharp, furious look.

I can't seem to find it here, Emmi, perhaps you have the telegram in your files –

Emmi No, I have never seen such a telegram.

David Major, if you tell me where the telegram is –

Furtwängler You won't find it because no such telegram exists.

Ominous silence. Then, Arnold forces a boisterous laugh.

Arnold Well, I tried, you got to admit, I tried. I thought I might just trap you there, Wilhelm, but David here was a little too quick for me. Smart move, David. Smart move. No, I don't have the telegram, but I know it exists. And I just want to tell you. Wilhelm, we're going to keep looking for it because I happen to believe you sent it.

Furtwängler Then you are wrong.

Arnold is not pleased.

Arnold Art and politics, yeah, art and politics. Are you saying that touring abroad, conducting the Berlin Philharmonic Orchestra in foreign lands from 1933 on, wasn't a commercial for Adolf and all he stood for?

Furtwängler We never, never officially represented the regime when we played abroad. We always played as a private ensemble. As I think I already told you, I was a freelance conductor –

Arnold You know something? You should've written our policies for us because you got more exclusion clauses than Double Indemnity. Don't give me fine print again, I'm an expert when it comes to fine print. What d'you imagine people thought? The Berlin Philharmonic's taken over by Josef's Propaganda Ministry but Wilhelm's a freelance, so music and politics are now entirely separate? Is that what you believed ordinary people thought?

Furtwängler I have no idea what ordinary people thought –

Arnold No –

Furtwängler – because I had only one intention, from 1933 onwards. Whatever I did, and this is also the real reason I did not leave my country, I had only one intention and that was to prove that art means more than politics.

Arnold Did that include Herbert von Karajan?

Furtwängler (*flustered*) What – what – I don't know what you mean –

Arnold Tell me about von der Nüll.

Furtwängler (*taken off guard*) Von der Nüll?

Arnold Yes, von der Nüll –

Furtwängler Von der Nüll –

Arnold How long's this going to go on, Wilhelm? I say von der Nüll, you say von der Nüll, I say von der Nüll, you say von der Nüll, we could go on all day. You know who von der Nüll is, don't you? Edwin von der Nüll, music critic –

Furtwängler Yes, I know who he is –

Arnold Isn't it true that because he gave you bad reviews and praised this young guy, von Karajan, called him a goddam miracle, said he was better than you, you had

von der Null conscripted into the army and nobody's
heard from him since?

Furtwängler That's an outrageous lie!

Arnold You sure you didn't call one of your close buddies
and say, 'God in heaven, did you see what that guy von
der Null wrote about me? I want him out the way'? And
the same with that other critic, Steinhauer. 'He had the
nerve to accuse me, the greatest conductor on earth, of not
playing enough modern music. Send him to Stalingrad.'
Isn't that what you did? You don't like criticism, do you?
You certainly didn't like them saying there was another
conductor who was better than you –

Furtwängler rises angrily. Exploding, pacing:

Furtwängler Please stop playing these games with me.
You seem to take pleasure in teasing and baiting and
hectoring me. Have some regard for my intelligence.
We are dealing here with matters concerning my entire
existence, my career, my life. Why you should introduce
the name of – of another conductor is beyond my
understanding.

Arnold I'll tell you why. You remember we talked about
you playing for Adolf's birthday? And you told me that
Josef got to your doctors first, that you were tricked,
outflanked?

Furtwängler Yes, and that's what happened –

Arnold I have a different story to tell. I don't believe
you were tricked. Not in the way you describe. I believe
something else happened. I've looked at the Hinkel
Archive, made a few enquiries, I've seen records of phone
calls, and putting it all together, this is what I think
happened. I think Josef said, 'Wilhelm, if you won't
conduct for Adolf's birthday, we'll get the Miracle Kid,

the guy that critic von der Null thinks is the greatest
conductor in the world, the guy you call K. He's not just
willing to conduct for Adolf, he's offered to sing "Happy
Birthday" as a solo.'

Silence.

Come on now, Wilhelm, admit it. K worried you, didn't
he? He always worried you. In 1942, he's thirty-four
years old, you're already fifty-six. He's the Young
Pretender, the comet, yeah, the miracle. He's tilting at
your throne. Your position's in danger. And Josef and
Hermann keep saying to you, 'If you don't do it, little
K will.' Never mind art and politics and symbols and
airy-fairy bullshit about liberty, humanity and justice.
You were tricked all right, because they got you where
you were most vulnerable. Youth was knocking on the
door, and I don't care how great you are, how noble,
how fantastic with your little white stick, because it's
the oldest story in the book. The ageing Romeo jealous
of the young buck, the Heavyweight Champion of the
World frightened of the Young Contender. And the great
Maestro terrified of the new boy on the podium. Wasn't
that how they got you, Wilhelm, time after time? Admit it.
The real reason you didn't leave the country when you
knew you should have was that you were frightened. You
were frightened that, once you were out of the way, you'd
be supplanted by the Miracle Kid, the Party's boy twice
over, flashy, talented little K.

Furtwängler This is absolute nonsense –

David Major, wait a moment, where is this leading? This
isn't establishing –

Arnold (*turning on him, cutting him off*) Not now,
David, I haven't finished with him. As a matter of fact,
I've hardly begun. I'm only just developing my theme.

Isn't that what you call it in classical music, developing a theme? Okay, Wilhelm, so they played on your insecurity. That's human, understandable, nothing to be ashamed of. After all, it's pretty well agreed that little K's got what it takes, and nearly everyone in the Party loved him. Jesus, he's a member twice over, he's one of theirs. But, take note of what I said. I said nearly everyone in the Party because there's one exception. One guy doesn't like little K as much as he likes you, there's one guy who thinks little K is not fit to brush your coat tails, and that guy just happens to be – yeah, the number-one man, your old pal, Adolf. He thinks you're the greatest and when he says, 'I want Wilhelm for my birthday party,' boy, they better go get Wilhelm. So, Josef calls and threatens you with little K. And you said, 'To hell with the Ninth in Vienna, I'll give it to Adolf as a birthday present in Berlin.' That's the trick they played, they got you by the balls and they squeezed. Hard.

David Major, I simply can't see how this line of questioning –

Arnold (*turning on him*) David, what is this? What are you all of a sudden, Counsel for the Defence? What you want me to say? Objection overruled? Objection sustained? My line of questioning is establishing motive, Counsellor, plain, ordinary human motive. Why did he stay? Why did he play for them? Why was he the flag-carrier for the regime? Why was he their servant? Not art or culture or music and its mystical power, but good old-fashioned insecurity, fear and jealousy. And that was only part of his reason for staying –

Furtwängler (*suddenly interrupting, blurting out*) Of course there was a conspiracy against me, a campaign. They controlled the press. Every word that was written, every word that was published. When I resigned from the

Philharmonic, when I refused to take part in a film they
made about the orchestra, oh, countless things of that
kind, refusing to co-operate in one way or another, they
were determined to keep me in my place. You mentioned
the critic, Edwin von der Null. His praise of – of – that
man may have been genuine, I have no idea. But his
remarks were encouraged and guided, and then seized on.
They wanted another 'star', as they called it, to take my
place. They had their own concert agency under a man
called Rudolf Vedder, a human being beneath contempt.
He was determined to foist K on the public. I'm not going
to recount the difficulties I had with that man, but if I tell
you that his chief ally in this was Ludolf von Alvensleben,
personal adjutant to Heinrich Himmler, and when that
particular individual did not get his way he threatened
only one sanction: death. They controlled every aspect
of our lives. They manipulated, bullied and imposed their
monstrous will. When they finally understood that I would
do everything in my power to prevent art from being
directed and supervised, they determined to undermine
me. They regarded any action of dissent, however small,
as a criticism of the state, tantamount to high treason.

Arnold And you didn't have von der Null conscripted
because of that review he wrote?

Furtwängler (*blazing*) I've told you, it's absolute nonsense.
How could I have managed such a thing? He was in their
power, not mine. It's a total lie. And I have never in my
life tried or even wanted to silence my critics, never. I
believe serious criticism to be an essential part of cultural
life. (*Turning to David; becoming excited.*) And the
reason you have detected a certain distaste I have for K is
not because I was jealous or insecure but because I have
serious criticism to make of him. In my opinion, he is an
intellectual conductor. He does not experience the piece

154

afresh each time. He conducts only what he knows and wants, in other words the nuances, which is why the nuances are all exaggerated. The slow tempi are too slow, the fast ones too fast. The whole effect is somewhat hysterical – (*He falls silent.*)

Arnold Wilhelm, I'm trying to understand you, I really am, believe me. You see, when you talk about cultural life. I'm lost. Because I am, to put it at its best, totally uncultured. So when I look at you, I don't see the great artist, the greatest conductor alive, I see a man, an ordinary guy, like a million other ordinary guys. And I ask myself, what keeps him in a situation which he says he did everything in his power to resist, except get the hell out of it? What keeps him here, I ask myself? Not being a cultured guy, I don't buy all this stuff about music preserving liberty, justice and humanity. I look for ordinary reasons, reasons I can understand, reasons my buddies can understand. So, if I said to my buddies, imagine you love your wife – well, maybe I'm stretching reality here – no, stay with me – I say to them, imagine you love your wife and they tell you you're being sent overseas. But they exempt some young guy who it's possible could take your wife's fancy. What would you do? Like a man they'd say, Steve, we'd do everything we could to stay put. See, Wilhelm, I'm talking about ordinary, everyday motives. Which is why I want to discuss your private life.

David Oh, come along, Major, this can't be right –

Arnold (*quietly*) Objection overruled, Counsellor. I'm establishing motive. (*To Furtwängler.*) How many illegitimate children do you have?

David Major, this is outrageous, what has this to do with anything at all?

Arnold You'll see. Wilhelm, did you hear the question?

Furtwängler (*barely audible*) I have illegitimate children –

Arnold What?

Furtwängler I said I have illegitimate children. I don't know how many.

Arnold No, I bet you don't. Four, five, six?

   No response.

You like the ladies, don't you, Wilhelm?

   No response.

Isn't it true that before every concert you got a woman in your dressing room and gave her the old conductor's baton, isn't that true?

David Major, this is deeply offensive and repugnant –

Arnold You bet –

David – and totally irrelevant.

Arnold Not so, Counsellor. The women threw themselves at you, didn't they, Wilhelm? That secretary of yours, Berta Geissmar, who's now working for *Sir* Thomas Beecham, she wasn't only your secretary, she was your procuress, wasn't she? She procured women for you, didn't she, as many and as often as you wanted –

Furtwängler Stop this, please, stop this –

Arnold No, I'm not going to stop it, because if I said to my buddies, you're living in a whorehouse where you get the whores free, you going to leave? See, Wilhelm, I think you stayed because you were in paradise here. Adolf himself offered you a beautiful house and a special bomb shelter –

Furtwängler I absolutely refused the house and the bomb shelter –

Arnold But you see what I'm getting at? You didn't stay because you felt an affinity with your people, or because you wanted to preserve the traditions of which, I think you said, you were a guardian, or because you believed that art and music and culture were above politics. See, if I said to my buddies, you're top dog in your profession, favourite of the number-one man in the country, you get all the women you lust after, you're highly paid, you get a gorgeous house and a personal, private bomb shelter if you want it, what you going to do, leave or stay? One voice comes back at me: stay!

David That's not a good argument, Major. If Dr Furtwängler did indeed enjoy all these – these privileges – he enjoyed them because of who he is and what he is.

Arnold Now we're back to the great artist –

David Right. His position would have guaranteed him anything he wanted wherever he chose to live and work. That's true of any leading artist in any country in the world. They're rare specimens, Major, and that sets them apart –

Arnold Okay, but it doesn't make them saints. They still have to get up and piss in the middle of the night, don't they? And they can be envious and vindictive and mean just like you and me. Well, just like me. Can't they?

No response.

See, Wilhelm, everybody says what a great benefactor you were to the Jews, but what about that Italian conductor?

Furtwängler I don't understand what you're talking about, but if you're now referring to Arturo Toscanini,

157

he is not a Jew, of course, but he is greatly loved by you Americans –

Arnold No, I was thinking of another Italian –

Furtwängler (*not hearing Arnold; again addressing David, rather over-excitedly*) – and to my taste, he is too disciplined, his tempi are too strict. If he were a greater artist, if he had deeper insights, a livelier imagination, greater warmth and devotion to the work, he would not have become so disciplined. This is why his success is disastrous. Inspiration and understanding in art are more important than discipline and autocratic behaviour.

Arnold But otherwise you like the guy. (*He chuckles.*) I'm beginning to get the picture. You're not crazy about any of your rivals, are you? I guess it was the same with this other Italian, the one I was thinking of, de Sabata –

Furtwängler De Sabata?

Arnold Vittorio de Sabata. I have a letter here, written in 1939, which states: (*Reading.*) 'What should I do when Dr Furtwängler said to me that it was a piece of impudence for that Jew de Sabata to conduct Brahms. Since the day when de Sabata performed *Tristan* in Bayreuth, Furtwängler speaks only of "Jew Sabata".'

Furtwängler Who wrote that letter?

Arnold I'm not at liberty to tell you that. But it's a genuine letter. David, you have a copy in the file, it's a genuine letter.

Furtwängler There's only one thing I can say. I have never said anything that goes counter to my convictions and simply cannot have said anything that did. Of course there were instances when I was speaking to specific Party members. I had to use their language, one had to say 'Heil Hitler', for example, but quite apart from these instances, I did not make any compromises by saying things other than I believed. And I have always been frank in my attitude towards the Jews –

Arnold I believe that. But just answer the question, don't give me explanations –

Furtwängler But I have to explain. An attitude must exist in one to make such an outburst possible. And this is what I deny. I know that even in the greatest anger I couldn't have said such a thing. De Sabata was my friend, one of my few close friends. I invited him to conduct my orchestra. We discussed his programme, we discussed everything –

Arnold Okay, so, here's another letter, July 4th, 1933, written by you to the Minister of Culture, Bernhard Rust. It's about this modern composer, a Jew, Arnold Schönberg, who was about to be suspended. There's a copy of this one, too, in your file, David. This is what you wrote, Wilhelm. (*Reading.*) 'Arnold Schönberg is considered by the Jewish International as the most significant musician of the present. It must be recommended that he not be made a martyr.' What do you say to that?

Furtwängler I say exactly what I said before. You have to use their language –

David And you didn't finish the letter, Major. (*Reading.*) 'And if he is suspended now – and I would not indeed consider this right – the question of indemnity should be treated with generosity.' He's pleading for the man, not condemning him –

Arnold Then what about these things he said? 'Jewish penpushers should be removed from the Jewish press,' 'Jewish musicians lack a genuine affinity with *our* music,' and 'Jewish musicians are good businessmen with few scruples, lacking roots.' You deny you said these things?

Furtwängler But it depends on the circumstances, to whom one was speaking – these attitudes simply don't exist in me, I used their language, of course I did, everyone did.

David Major, you have to balance those things – if indeed he said them – against his assistance to his Jewish colleagues. Listen to this, Major, from the transcript of the proceedings at Nürnberg –

Arnold (*enjoying this*) Okay, Counsellor, here we go, it's your day in court. But be careful, there's nothing I enjoy more than a guy putting his own neck in the noose.

David A Swedish businessman, Birger Dahlerus, testified in cross-examination that he had several meetings with Hermann Göring. 'I first saw Göring,' Dahlerus testified, 'embroiled in a stormy interview with Wilhelm Furtwängler, the famous conductor of the Berlin Philharmonic, who was vainly seeking permission to keep his Jewish concert master.'

Furtwängler Yes, I remember well, I was pleading for Szymon Goldberg, a wonderful musician and a wonderful man, the youngest Konzertmeister the orchestra ever had. Thank God he escaped, and I pray that he is safe now –

Arnold Why is it, Wilhelm, that everything you say touches me so deeply?

David (*flaring*) Emmi, read one of those letters to Mrs Sachs. Pick any one, read it –

> *Emmi, uncertain, looks at Arnold, who, indifferent, gestures for her to do as she's been told. She selects a letter at random.*

Emmi I can't decipher this signature, but – (*Reading.*)
'Please remember that helping Jews was a capital offence.
People were being publicly hanged on mere suspicion of
such activities but Dr Furtwängler helped anyone who
asked him. I personally testify to having seen literally
hundreds of people lined up outside his dressing room
after concerts to ask for his help. He never turned anyone
away. He gave me money because I was unable to feed
myself or my family and then he helped me to escape to
Sweden. He helped countless people in similar ways.'

David Doesn't sound like much of an anti-Semite to me,
Major. These are acts of enormous courage –

Arnold (*smiling*) You don't listen to what I say, David.
How many times have I got to tell you I was in insurance?
You think I can't smell a phoney policy when it's shoved
under my nose? Sure, he helped Jews, but that was just
insurance, his cover, because the whole time he was
Maestro of all he surveyed. (*Turning to Furtwängler.*) See,
Wilhelm, I think you're cunning, devious, dealing off the
bottom of the pack. You were their boy, their creature.
That's the case against you, old pal. You were like an
advertising slogan for them. This is what we produce,
the greatest conductor in the world. And you went along
with it. You may not have been a member of the Party
because the truth is, Wilhelm, you didn't need to be. (*To
Emmi.*) Emmi, put that record on –

*Emmi puts on the record of the Adagio from Bruckner's
Seventh Symphony.*

Arnold You know what that is?

Furtwängler Of course I know what that is –

Arnold Okay, so what is it?

Furtwängler The Seventh Symphony of Anton Bruckner.
The Adagio.

Arnold Who's conducting?

Furtwängler I am.

Arnold You know the last time it was played on these
airwaves?

Furtwängler How should I know such a thing?

Arnold Well then, I'll tell you. The last time this music
was played on these airwaves was after they announced
that your pal Adolf had blown his brains out. Listen
to it.

They listen.

Did they pick little K's recording? Did they pick some
other band leader? No, they picked you, and why? Because
you and nobody else represented them so beautifully.
When the Devil died they wanted his band leader to play
the funeral march. (*He takes off the record.*) You were
everything to them.

Furtwängler I have always tried – I have tried to analyse
myself closely. You are right, Major. I am no better than
anybody else. But I must always say what my instincts
are. In staying here, I believed – I thought – I walked a
tightrope between exile and the gallows. You seem to be
blaming me for not having allowed myself to be hanged.
I tried to defend the intellectual life of my people against
an evil ideology. I did not directly oppose the Party
because, I told myself, this was not my job. I would have
benefited no one by active resistance. But I never hid my
opinions. As an artist I was determined that music, at
least, would remain untouched, untainted. If I had taken
any active part in politics I couldn't have remained here.

Please understand me correctly: an artist cannot be entirely
apolitical. He must have some political convictions because
he is, after all, a human being. As a citizen, it is an artist's
duty to express these convictions. But as a musician, I am
more than a citizen. I am a citizen of this country in that
eternal sense to which the genius of great music testifies.
I know that a single performance of a great masterpiece
was a stronger and more vital negation of the spirit of
Buchenwald and Auschwitz than words. Human beings
are free wherever Wagner and Beethoven are played.
Music transported them to regions where the torturers
and murderers could do them no harm.

> *Arnold grabs the baton from his desk, stands
> trembling before Furtwängler, and snaps it in half.
> Emmi puts her fingers in her ears.*

Arnold (*his rage erupting with quiet, terrifying menace*)
Have you ever smelled burning flesh? I smelt it four miles
away. Four miles away, I smelt it. I smell it now, I smell
it at night because I can't sleep any more with the stench
of it in my nostrils. I'll smell it for the rest of my life.
Have you seen the crematoria and the gas ovens? Have
you seen the mounds of rotting corpses being shovelled
into gigantic craters by the men and women who murdered
them? I saw these things with my own eyes. And I've seen
it every night since, night after night, and I wake screaming
seeing it. I know I won't sleep undisturbed ever again.
You talk to me about culture and art and music? You
putting that in the scales, Wilhelm? You setting culture
and art and music against the millions put to death by
your pals? The pals you could call to save a couple of
Jews when thousands, millions of them, were being
annihilated? Is that what you're putting on the scales?
Yes, I blame you for not getting hanged, I blame you for
your cowardice. You strutted and swaggered, king-pin

in a shithouse. You talk to me of walking a tightrope
between exile and the gallows, and I say to you, lies –

Furtwängler (*breaking down*) I love my country, I believe
in art, what was I to do?

Arnold Act courageously. Just think of real courage, think
of what men like Emmi's father did, risking their lives,
not their careers –

He sees Emmi has her fingers in her ears, yells at her.

For Chrissake, Emmi, take your goddam fingers out of
your ears –

She does so, tense, strained.

I'm talking about your father, I'm talking about real
courage, I'm talking about him risking his fucking life –

*She screams, the chilling sound of one who can take
no more. All stare at her, shocked.*

Emmi My father only joined the plot when he realised
we could not win the war.

Furtwängler Major, what kind of a world do you want?
What kind of world are you going to make? Don't you
honestly understand the power of art to communicate
beauty and pain and triumph? Even if you can't admit it,
don't you believe that music especially transcends language
and national barriers and speaks directly to the human
spirit? If you honestly believe the only reality is the physical
world, you will have nothing left but feculence more
foul-smelling than that which pervades your nights –
(*Near to breakdown.*) This isn't just, this isn't fair. How
was I to know what they were capable of? No one knew.
No one knew they were gangsters, atrocious, depraved.
(*He breaks down, buries his face in his hands.*) Oh God,
I don't want to stay in this country. Yes, yes, it would

have been better if I'd left in 1934, it would have been better if I'd left –

He suddenly retches. Emmi goes to him.

Arnold (*yelling*) Helmuth!

Rode comes to the door.

Show your friend to the toilet and then tell him to get the hell out of here.

Rode and Emmi help Furtwängler.

Emmi, Helmuth can manage –

Emmi ignores him and exits with Rode and Furtwängler. Arnold marches to the telephone table, sits, lifts the receiver and dials.

David You know what, Major? We'll never understand. Only tyrannies understand the power of art. I wonder how I would have behaved in his position? I'm not certain I'd have 'acted courageously'. And what about you, Major? I have a feeling we might just have followed orders.

Arnold I'm only a claims assessor. Who cares about me? But everyone kept telling me your man was something special. And you know what? He's not special at all.

David You know what I say he is, Major?

Arnold No, what do you say he is, David?

David I say he's like a fallen priest –

Arnold (*into telephone*) Alex Vogel. (*To David.*) And what would you know about priests, Lieutenant Vile?

David (*a smile*) Only what I read in books.

Arnold Yeah, and what did you read?

David That they can be inadequate human beings. They can lie, they can fornicate, they can drink, they can deceive. But they can still put God into the mouths of the faithful. If you believe in that sort of thing.

David goes to the record player, removes the Bruckner, finds another record.

Arnold You know what I say you are, David?

David I know what you say I am, Major.

Arnold Yeah, but you're worse. You're a liberal piece of shit. You don't know right from wrong.

Emmi returns, slightly dazed, holding a visitor's card.

Emmi (*to David, quietly*) He thanked me and gave me his visiting card.

David half smiles, puts the other record on the turntable.

Arnold (*into the telephone*) Vogel? Arnold. I don't know if we've got a case that'll stand up, but we can sure as hell give him a hard time –

At full volume the sound of the subdued opening of Beethoven's Ninth Symphony.

(*To David.*) Hey, turn that off – can't you see I'm on the phone? (*Into the telephone.*) Yeah, yeah, but it makes no – Never mind, we got a tame journalist who'll write what we'll tell him. (*Listens.*) Yeah, a guy called Delbert Clark, *New York Times* –

The great chords sound.

Jesus Christ, what the hell are you doing? Turn that goddam thing down –

But David ignores him, sits, implacable, listening.
Furtwängler stumbles into the bomb rubble, as if a
broken man struggling to regain his composure.

Turn it off!

In the rubble, Furtwängler hears the music but he
cannot identify its source. His left hand trembles but it
is only his way of sensing the tempo. After a while the
music and the lights begin to fade to:

Blackout.